BASIC
BUDGETING *for*
CHURCHES

BASIC BUDGETING *for* CHURCHES

A COMPLETE GUIDE

JACK A. HENRY

BROADMAN
&HOLMAN
PUBLISHERS

Nashville, Tennessee

4261-75
0-8054-6175-2

Dewey Decimal Classification: 254.8
Subject Heading: Church \ Finance
Library of Congress Card Catalog Number: 94-23532

Unless otherwise noted, all Scripture quotations
are from the King James Version of the Bible.

MoneyCounts® is a registered trademark of Parsons Technology, Inc. The MoneyCounts software and documentation are property of Parsons Technology, Inc., copyright ©1985–94 by Parsons Technology, Inc., all rights reserved. Parsons Technology, 1 Parsons Dr., P.O. Box 100, Hiawatha, IA 52233-0100. For ordering information, call 1-800-223-6925.

Page Compositor: Trina D. Hollister

Library of Congress Cataloging-in-Publication Data
Henry, Jack A.
Basic budgeting for churches : a complete guide / by Jack A. Henry
    p. cm.
ISBN 0-8054-6175-2
Includes index.
1. Church finance. 2. Budget. I. Title.
BV774.5.H46   1995
  254.8—dc20
                        94-23532
                        CIP

5 05 04 03 02

To the many pastors and members
of church budget committees
who labor hard and long
to stretch every ministry dollar
their church receives—
and whose efforts are
often unappreciated.

Contents

Introduction

For which of you, intending to build a tower, sitteth not down first, and counteth the cost, whether he have sufficient to finish it?

Lest haply, after he hath laid the foundation, and is not able to finish it, all that behold it begin to mock him,

Saying, This man began to build, and was not able to finish.

—*Luke 14:28–30*

Getting Started

Pastors and churches seldom have all of the money they would like to have to do what they want for God. Sometimes pastors and churches excuse their lack of accomplishments for God by telling themselves that they have done the best they could with what they have—and sometimes that is not entirely true. The entire truth may be that they have done the best they know how to do; but because they do not know how to develop and operate a simple budget, they have missed the "best" and have settled for the "best they know how."

This book is written for the new pastor, or one who is going to start a new church. It will also be very helpful to the experienced pastor or a member of a church

Because [many pastors and churches] do not know how to develop and operate a simple budget, they have missed the "best" and have settled for the "best they know how."

finance committee who may not be experienced in developing and using budgets.

Sometimes a pastor may say that there is no way he can develop a budget because he cannot know how much the offerings will be—he just spends what comes in. Other pastors may say, "I know what the church needs, so I just spend what comes in on what the church needs." If you ask him how much he thinks will come in to cover the church's expenses, he will tell you. When he tells you he knows the church's needs and how much he thinks will come in to cover them, he is really telling you about his budget—he just is not calling it that.

Tools for Planning

Recognizing that a pastor's time must be free for visitation, evangelism, Bible study, and prayer, the procedures taught in this book are not excessively time consuming and allow the maximum amount of time for the other duties of the ministry. They will, however, provide the pastor and church the necessary tools for planning for the best use of the money God gives them and for insuring that the plan works.

The first chapter outlines the budget basics—the what and why of developing a church budget. The role of the pastor and church members in setting objectives for the church and the relationship of church objectives to the budget and its operation will be discussed so that their interrelationship can be seen and understood.

After gaining an appreciation of the need for budgeting and its relationship to the ministry of the church, we will move on to the work of developing a budget in chapter 2. The requirements for a good budget, where to get the information needed, and the process that is involved in its preparation and approval will be presented in chapter 3. Because the budget approval process varies according to the size and organizational structure of each congregation, basic procedures and their application in different situations will be illustrated.

When talking about budgets, the annual budget is usually what is meant. However, in order to have enough money to pay bills on a timely basis, we must also develop a budget that shows how much money we expect to come in each month so we will know how much we will have available to spend each month. This is called a cash flow budget and is discussed in chapter 4. After developing the plan for the year, we will see how to use that information to develop a plan for cash flow.

Many people, pastors included, do not think very highly of budgets or budgeting because they do not use them effectively after they develop them. In chapter 5 we will discuss procedures for making a budget "work" and also cover ways the budget can help us handle emergencies and take advantage of unexpected opportunities.

One function of money management that is often overlooked is spending. Some churches keep good records and are meticulous in their budgeting procedures, yet they lose the benefits of substantial sums of money because they have loose spending procedures. After completing our discussion of the budget and its role in church financial management, we will discuss the control of spending in chapter 6. Included in our discussion of spending will be receiving procedures and the use of purchase orders.

Computers can help us keep the financial records required for good financial management; they are the topic of chapter 7. They can also provide substantial help in budget development and operation. Ways in which inexpensive, basic computer hardware and software can be used to enhance churches' budgeting processes are included.

It's Easy

Budgets are not just for big churches, or rich churches. Budgets are for all churches that want to use the resources God gives them to the best advantage.

Budgeting does not require clairvoyance, mathematical genius, nor computer wizardry. Church budgeting only requires you to have a Holy Spirit-led mind to discern God's goals for your congregation; a yielded heart to acknowledge His leadership; the courage to walk by faith toward the goals God places before you—and the ability to add, subtract, multiply, and divide.

Chapter 1

*And he said unto another, Follow me. But he said, Lord,
suffer me first to go and bury my father.*

*Jesus said unto him, Let the dead bury their dead: but go
thou and preach the kingdom of God.*

*And another also said, Lord, I will follow thee: but let me
first go bid them farewell, which are at home at my house.*

*And Jesus said unto him, No man, having put his hand
to the plow, and looking back, is fit for the kingdom of God.*

—Luke 9:59–62

Budget Basics

The Lord reminds believers to "count the cost" before beginning to build a tower to make sure we have enough to finish (Luke 14:28–30). He also tells us that we need to set priorities in our life—and in our use of our resources—because all things are not of equal importance nor need to be done at the same time. The Lord did not say that what these young men who wanted to be His disciples asked to do was wrong; He just said that burying their dead and saying good-bye were not the highest priorities in their lives. He reminded them that they needed to keep their eyes on the main goal and do first things first.

> We often fall short of accomplishing what God wants us to do because we do not get our priorities straight.

The Lord has plenty of work to be done—everyone can have a job; His is a "full-employment" economy. However, we often fall short of accomplishing what God wants us to do because we do not get our priorities straight. Budgets and budgeting require us to know what we can do and what our priorities are among all of the options.

What Is a Budget?

A budget is a plan for allocating available resources. We usually talk about money when we refer to budgets, but we could use the same definition regarding allocation of any resource; i.e., a time budget, or space budget. Budgeting money is simply a matter of setting priorities on everything that you want to do so that the money is used for the most important things *first*. By doing that, no matter how much or how little money you have to spend, you will always do the most important things with your money.

One prominent misconception about budgets is that there is some magic way they help you decide how to spend your money. There is no magic. You cannot escape the task of making decisions. The budget process will help you make sure that you consider all alternatives, but you have to make the decisions about which one is funded first, second, and so on. You have to decide what is going to get done and what is not going to get done if you do not have all of the money you need to pay for everything you want to do. Budgets are not developed to exclude faith from our actions. They are the result of reasoned decisions—arrived at by faith—about what God wants you to do with the financial resources He has given you.

Since a budget is defined as a plan to allocate available resources, the need to know four things is implied:

1. How much money will be available to spend?
2. What needs to be done?
3. How much will it cost to accomplish each need?
4. What is the order of priority among the things that need to be done?

We often waste time and money because we put off making spending decisions until we are faced with an emergency, or we are trapped with no possibility for

> A budget is a plan for allocating available resources. . . .[It] is simply a matter of setting priorities . . . so that the money is used for the most important things *first*.

> Budgets are the result of reasoned decisions—arrived at by faith—about what God wants you to do with the financial resources He has given you.

further procrastination. Decision making is hard work and requires prayer and research, prayer and reflection, and prayer and action. Budgeting requires decision making, so budgeting is hard work.

Budgeting requires decision making, so budgeting is hard work.

It is easy to get into the habit of making decisions on the spur of the moment and without adequate research or reflection. Arriving at a truly workable spending plan that the Lord can bless is much more likely if you:

1. Do research in a timely way

2. Reflect on the various relationships of one part of the ministry to another (one part of the budget to another)

3. Bathe every consideration in prayer.

The budget is a "road map" to help you get from where you are to where you are going financially. It helps you stay on the road and not "get lost." If you get off course because of some financial setback, whether it be lower income than expected or an unplanned expense, your budget helps you see where you are in relation to where you want to be. This knowledge enables you to develop a plan to get back on the road to your goal.

The budget is a "road map" to help you get from where you are to where you are going financially. It helps you stay on the road and not "get lost."

Sometimes a church will court financial disaster by throwing out their budget when they run into difficulties instead of using it to help reach their original goals. Usually the original goals and priorities have not changed; there has just been a change in the amounts of either their income or expenses. Using the same procedures they used in developing their budget in the first place—prayer and research, prayer and reflection, and prayer and action—they can adjust for any difficulty that may arise.

Your budget should be only a "guide" and not the "master" of your fate. After all, you are the one who decided which road to take in the first place. If you made it, you can change it. Budgets should not be changed capriciously, but they can and should be changed when events, both good and bad, dictate a need for change. If you find that you must take a detour, then plan to take the shortest route around the problem and back onto your original route as soon as possible.

Not only does a budget serve as a guide; it also helps evaluate how you are doing. Just as you like to know if you are making good progress and will get to your destination on time when you travel, you also need to know if you are making good progress toward your church's financial goals and if you can expect to reach them as planned. Your church goals are stated in terms of ministry, but you must have the financial capacity to accomplish them. Having a budget gives you a means of comparing your actual financial progress with your plan. When you are making progress as planned, you can rejoice. When you are getting behind, you can make adjustments. When you are running ahead of schedule, you can plan to take on more ministries with the excess money.

> Not only does a budget serve as a guide; it also helps you evaluate how you are doing.

What Does a Budget Do for You?

Your budget can be one of your most important motivational aids for securing the support for all of your church's ministries. Since a budget puts a "dollars and cents" value on every activity of the church, it reflects your priorities—you will spend money on the things you believe are most important. You will discuss each ministry of your church with your finance committee and the church as a whole as you develop the budget and secure its approval. While doing that, you will have a chance to enlist the support of the members and recruit workers for every ministry as you discuss its part in the overall budget.

> Since your budget puts a "dollars and cents" value on every activity of the church, it reflects your priorities—you will spend money on the things you believe are important.

After making your budget choices, you will find that they will guide your actions so that you will not be faced with daily "Should I?" or "Should I not?" spending decisions. Your daily spending activity will already be laid out for you. You will not have to worry about making those annoying little spending decisions that can eat up time that should be devoted to other activities. You not only will save time and use money more wisely, but you will enjoy the freedom you gain from having spending decisions already made.

Tithing is a good illustration of how making spending decisions in advance frees you from having to make repeated decisions. When you decided to be obedient to the Lord by tithing, you made a "budget decision." You decided that the first tenth of your income was going to the Lord. After making that one decision, you do not have to decide every Sunday if you are going to give something—or how much—to the Lord's work. You already made the decision, so all you have to do is carry it out.

Budgets control the actions of the people who are responsible for spending church funds in the sense that budgets make the limits clear. To the extent that they are committed to working within the budget guidelines, people are controlled by the budget. You must not get carried away, however, with the idea that budgets control people—they don't. Budgets guide people, but people control budgets.

Budgets guide people, but people control budgets.

The very act of developing a budget forces you to evaluate past spending habits and to decide what you are going to do in the future. You are also forced to make decisions and establish priorities for all of the possible ministries your church may undertake during the coming year. These very acts, in themselves, not only help you develop better budgets that give you more freedom in your daily work, they also help you see God's blessings and guiding hand.

Budgets and Church Objectives

Every facet of church activity needs to be considered when developing your budget.

Every facet of church activity needs to be considered when developing your budget—the people, the buildings, the equipment, the buses, the Sunday School, the visitation program, the music program, the youth program, the fellowship activities and the spiritual activities. Everything that your church does or is planning to do should be written down and considered when developing your church budget.

Although the major part of the church budget probably originates in the pastor's heart, do not rule out the possibility that God may have given you people to minister to who also have a burning desire to minister. Do not forget that God did not call you to do the work of the church; He assigned the work of the church to the church—His people.

The people who lead or participate in some ministry of your church may have objectives for their own ministries that you would wholeheartedly support, but their needs will not get put into the church budget if you do not ask for their input. Remember, a budget indicates the priorities assigned to all of the church's ministries, not just the pastor's ministry—and you have to know about all of the potential ministries before you can set priorities.

Summary

Your church budget is your plan for how you are going to spend the money you receive during the coming year. It requires research, prayer, and decision making.

If you are going to achieve the most you can with what you have, you will have to consider all of the possible ministries for the coming year and decide which ones you can do and which ones you cannot do.

Not only will you have to decide which ministries you will include in your church program, but you must also decide about the level of activity for each. Some programs cost little in money but require a great deal of volunteer effort. Others require little in manpower but have high, recurring financial demands. Can you afford both at the level desired for each? Or must you fully fund one ministry and partially fund the other? These are the questions that you must answer when making budget decisions.

Decision making is hard work for most people. Some pastors and laymen who are responsible for managing church money are natural procrastinators and have a hard time making up their minds; they just do whatever seems to be the easiest thing at the time.

Making decisions after thorough research and fervent prayer is much more likely to result in good decisions that will use the Lord's money to the greatest advantage.

Chapter 2

And Jesus answered and said unto her, Martha, Martha, thou art careful and troubled about many things:
But one thing is needful: and Mary hath chosen that good part, which shall not be taken away from her.
—*Luke 10:41–42*

Budget Development

Mary and Martha both had choices to make. They had different priorities, however, so they chose to use their time in different ways. Their "time budgets" were different, but each reflected the choices that had been made.

Two churches in the same area with similar membership, attendance, and offerings may have very dissimilar budgets because their choices about how to spend their money are not the same. Each budget will reflect the individual church's decisions about which ministries it will engage in and the priority of each ministry in relation to the others. There is no "right" budget, only a budget that is "right" for a specific church.

Two churches in the same area with similar membership, attendance, and offerings may have very dissimilar budgets because their choices about how to spend their money are not the same.

Beginning the Budget Process

Budgeting is a process, not an action. By that, I mean that a series of actions, or activities, takes place over a period of time that culminates in a budget. What many people consider to be "budgeting," that is the action of listing things to be bought or paid for and what each costs, is only one of the activities of the budgeting process. Budgeting also includes setting goals, assigning priorities to them, developing a plan for achieving them, operating the plan, evaluating the results, and replanning.

Developing a budget and getting it approved by the church are just the beginning of the budget process. After the budget has been approved, it must be used as planned and revised when necessary if it is to accomplish its purpose.

To develop a budget that is right for your church, you must do several things.

1. Set goals.
2. Establish priorities for each of them.
3. Estimate your income.
4. Estimate your expenses.
5. "Balance the Budget," or get the projected expenses equal to or lower than the projected income.

Setting Goals and Priorities

Since your budget is supposed to help you accomplish your goals, you must first decide what your goals are. Church budgets are usually developed to reflect the expected income and expenses for one year. Most churches use the calendar year for their fiscal year, so your first priority is to take time for prayer and reflection about what God wants for your church in the coming year.

Your financial goals for the year are often very basic, but they should be stated and written down so they will not be overlooked. Some goals might be to pay the mortgage and utility bills on time, begin paying the pastor a salary, begin supporting five new missionaries on a regular monthly basis by the end of the year, set aside $5,000 to be used to buy property when the opportunity presents itself, etc. One way to keep from overlooking any current ministry is to refer to your church's organizational chart, if you have one, to consider every aspect of the church's operation.

The only things you can manage are people, things, time, and space. Since your need for each of those four affects your need for money, you must consider all four when developing your budget.

Church goals begin in the pastor's heart. He is generally the first one to see opportunities for new ministries or recognize when old ministries should be eliminated. Leading the church is what God called him to do, and God guides him along the way.

> Church goals begin in the pastor's heart. . . . and God guides him along the way.

However, the pastor is not the only church member to whom God may be speaking about a ministry opportunity. Because of that, a way must be provided for every church member to have input during the budget development process. The pastor may see a need for a new ministry but not put it in the budget because he does not know how he could work it into his schedule. At the same time, God may be laying that ministry on the heart of one of the members and burdening him or her to volunteer to lead it. To improve the possibility that these two desires are brought together, well publicized channels of communication must be established and utilized so no ministry opportunity is overlooked.

After all goals have been identified, each one must be assigned a priority that places it in its proper relationship to all of the church's other ministry goals. You cannot "chicken out" here! If you are going to do the most important things with the money you receive, you must decide which are the most important—you must set priorities. Unless you set priorities, you are not making a budget—you are merely making a list of bills and dreams.

> After all goals have been identified, each one must be assigned a priority that places it in its proper relationship to all of the church's other ministry goals.

Remember, since your goals will change from year to year, you must stay flexible when budgeting. When you add new goals or drop old ones that are no longer appropriate, you have no trouble realizing that you are making a change and need to adjust other budget priorities. It is more difficult, however, to recognize the need for change when you are only reviewing some recurring budget item (line item). The tendency is to assume that the priorities and needs of these "standard" recurring budget items will stay the same or, at most, need only a change to cover inflation. The real facts may be that one or more of these standard budget items may need to be dropped or have its priority changed because of changed circumstances. For example, you may have added a full-time youth minister to your staff and now need to increase the amount of your travel and transportation budget so you can take advantage of the new potential gained by adding him. You can expect that a substantial change in one of the budget's line items will have a "ripple effect" and affect others, too.

The only way to insure that your budget truly reflects your current needs and priorities is to consider every budget item on its own merit each year, a technique called "Zero-Based Budgeting." Consider every budget item carried over from former years without assumptions about its priority or the amount needed. Every budget item should be justified on its own merits in relation to the circumstances of the new budget year. The justification for each item and the cost computations should be in written form. This allows them to be evaluated against what actually happens, so if circumstances change, budget changes can be made with minimum additional labor.

> The only way to insure that your budget truly reflects your current needs and priorities is to consider every budget item on its own merit each year, a technique called "Zero-Based Budgeting."

Estimating Income

Making financial estimates bothers many pastors. They feel unable to make adequate estimates of church income or expenses for the coming year because there are always so many variables to consider. However, since the pastor is usually the one with the most knowledge about the potential impact of each of those variables, he is also the best person to make the estimates.

An estimate is not a number that results from an exact calculation. An estimate is an opinion or judgment about what is considered most likely to happen. In other words, your estimate of your income for the next year represents your best, most reasoned judgment—your best guess. You will want your estimate to be as close to what actually happens as possible, so you must consider the impact of every variable that will affect it. Remember, however, you can never be exact when considering the total estimated church income.

If you are starting a new church, you have almost no data on which to base your income estimate, but you do have some. If you or your wife are going to be working, you know there will be at least one tithe envelope in the offering each week and you know approximately what that amount will be. Perhaps you have been promised financial support by sister churches to help you get started, and you will know the amount to plan on from them. Other sources of known income special to your situation also can be added to your data to make your estimate. Use the information you have and do the best you can—that is what an estimate is, your best reasoned guess.

Another source of information available to a pastor starting a new church is the advice of a pastor of a sister church in the area. He will be able to help you evaluate the estimate you made based on your data. He may even be able to help you make a reasonable estimate of the growth you can expect in your new congregation, including growth of financial contributions. Remember, however, that this information is another person's estimate; it is not financial data. You must make the final decision about your estimated income.

You may be starting a church as a mission of an already established church in your area. In that case, the pastor of the sponsoring church will have a great deal of information available to help develop your first budget. In some cases, the sponsoring church may control the development and operation of the budget of the mission church until it is ready to function on its own and is established as a new, separate church. In these situations, the pastor and other workers in the mission church are able to gain valuable experience in the entire budgeting process before they have to do it on their own. Even if the sponsoring church does not control the mission church's budget, it is a vital source of information of which the mission church should take advantage.

If you pastor an established church, your bookkeeping records are your best source of information for making income estimates. They give you exact information about what has happened in the past. By using that data, all you have to do is adjust it for the changes you expect for the coming year. Your estimate still will not be exact, but it can be very close if you carefully consider each of your ministries and how each one will affect your income.

If you use some kind of commitment card plan for financing your missions program, the card that each person completes and turns in gives you a solid basis for estimating your missions program income. Since each person makes a commitment to give a certain amount during the course of the next year, all you have to do to compute a preliminary estimate of missions income is to total the amount promised on each card. You still have work to do however; some churches always receive more than is promised on the cards, and some always receive less—you have to use your own judgment and make your own estimate of what to expect.

Churches also may receive promises, or pledges, from their members for other special purposes such as building programs; some also receive pledges for the general fund. In both cases, income estimates are easily made by following the same procedure outlined for missions.

When estimating income, always be conservative and round down. The standard advice is "only count on sure things." The problem is that there are no "sure things" when dealing with church income. When making estimates of income, you usually have a range of expected amounts; e.g., Missions Income $12,000–$15,000. Use the lowest amount when making your

If you pastor an established church, your bookkeeping records are your best source of information for making income estimates.

When estimating income, always be conservative and round down.

budget. If more than $12,000 is received, you can take on more missionary projects.

Estimating Expenses

As with income estimates, your estimates for expenses can never be exact. When estimating expenses, be liberal and round up—the opposite of what you did in estimating income. If you think something will cost between $500 and $600, use the higher figure.

Make a list of your "fixed expenses" and utilities and their costs before you begin working on the other expenses. Fixed expenses are regularly recurring in roughly the same amounts and are usually related to the church's general operation. Examples of fixed expenses are the mortgage payment or rent, salaries, and insurance. Utilities such as water, electricity, and phone vary in amount each month, but they are regular and recurring and must be paid. These costs often represent the major portion of your expenses and are usually high on your priority list.

After you estimate these costs, you have usually completed the majority of your budget's expense estimates. What is left—the difference between your estimated income and the amount of fixed expenses and utilities—is what you have available to divide among all of your ministry expenses. You seldom have enough left to fund all of the remaining ministries in the amounts you desire, so the priorities you established at the beginning of the budgeting process will determine how you conclude it.

Balancing the Budget

Many times people confuse the budget balancing step with budget operation—they think that budget balancing means staying within the budget. Actually, balancing the budget is part of the planning procedure and is merely the act of making sure that the planned expenditures are less than or equal to the planned income.

You can only do a good job of budgeting if you have considered all of your expected income and all of your

> When estimating expenses, be liberal and round up.

> Balancing the budget . . . is merely the act of making sure that the planned expenditures are less than or equal to the planned income.

desired expenditures. There is no such thing as "operating outside of the budget." If you overlook any income—perhaps an offering you are planning to take during the year for a special project—you will not have done your work of budgeting.

You may say to yourself, "But I'm going to spend the entire amount I raise on that special project, so it won't affect the budget." What you have done, in effect, is develop a separate budget for a special project. You have estimated the cost of the project and the amount of money you think you can raise to cover it—a budget. However, you have also exempted the project from being considered on its merits with all of the other ministries of the church. If you do not raise as much as you expect from the special offering, or if you have cost overruns, where will the additional money for the project come from? The answer is that it will come from funds that have been earmarked to cover other budget items.

Do not forget that a church is a single unit. As every member is a part of the body, the church, every activity and function is done by the body. You can develop "mini-budgets," or subsidiary budgets, for special ministries—you might have a Missions Budget, a Sunday School Budget, or a Youth Budget—but all of those "mini-budgets" should be included in the church's final, general budget.

When your estimated income from all sources and all desired ministries have been considered and their costs have been estimated, put them down on paper and add them up—this is your first draft of your budget. If your estimated income is more than your planned expenses, the budget is "out of balance." The excess of income above your planned expenses is called discretionary income and is available to be used for any purpose you might desire—this is when you can be creative. You may want to save the extra money in case some additional ministry opportunity presents itself during the course of the year. In that case, you might add a contingency fund to your budget for the amount that was excess (see app. B). Now the planned expenses will equal the planned income, and the budget is balanced.

For most new churches, and probably most older ones, too, there will be more ministries you need to fund than you can afford with your expected income. If you find yourself in that position, you will have to reduce expenses until they are no more than your planned income. The priorities you assigned at the beginning of the budgeting process will direct your efforts in reducing the planned expenses. You may have to eliminate whole programs, or you may be able to reduce or curtail the extent of some ministries to reduce their overall costs. Here, at the planning stage, when you have time to pray and reflect, is the time to make cuts in programs. Do not wait until later in the year after programs have been started and funds have been exhausted

For many pastors and church financial officers, this budget balancing procedure is skipped because it is very strenuous work, mentally and spiritually. Nobody wants to tell a fellow worker, "We cut your program." It is easier to put it off and hope you do not run out of money—after all, you tell yourself, if you run out of money, they will understand why you are cutting their program.

Hard work or not, the difference between a good budget that is useful and helpful and one that is just a "paper exercise" rests on whether the hard choices have been made. You cannot quit until you have a balanced budget that reflects your church's ministry plans for the coming year.

> At the planning stage, when you have time to pray and reflect, is the time to make cuts in programs, [not during] the year after programs have been started and funds have been exhausted.

> The difference between a good budget that is useful and helpful and one that is just a "paper exercise" rests on whether the hard choices have been made.

Requirements for a Good Budget

Edgar Walz says in his book, *Church Business Methods*, that there are five characteristics of a good budget. He says that an effective church budget should be complete, equitable, capable of change, attainable, and challenging.[1]

In this chapter's section on setting goals and priorities, and estimating income and expenditures, we dis-

---

1. Edgar Walz, *Church Business Methods* (St. Louis, Mo.: Concordia Publishing House, 1970), 53.

cussed the need for completeness. The subject of being equitable was discussed within the topic of assigning priorities. A budget does not have to allocate the same amount of funds to every ministry to be equitable, but it does need to allocate sufficient funds for each ministry to accomplish the goals that have been set for it. If the total amount of funds requested for a ministry is not allocated, review the expectations you have for that ministry and lower them if necessary since you are not funding them completely.

Remember, people control budgets, not the other way around.

A budget also needs to be flexible, or capable of change, during the period in which it is operating. Remember, people control budgets, not the other way around. Although budgets represent the church's best estimate of what will happen, emergencies may arise, or unexpected opportunities may present themselves that will require changes. When these events occur, your budget will help you decide where changes can be made best to adjust for the new circumstances. Your procedures for making adjustments are the same as those discussed in the section on balancing the budget, and they will be covered in more detail in chapter 5.

You assessed the attainability of your budget when you made your estimates of income and expenses. However, in addition to insuring that your budget is attainable, you should also consider if it is challenging to your people. Your budget should not be so large that it scares the congregation into believing it is beyond their capability, but it should be demanding enough to challenge them.

One of a church's scriptural purposes is to teach the members to walk by faith in obedience to God. This includes growing in dependence on God to supply their financial needs so they can give more to support the spiritual ministries of His church. If the ministries that are included in the budget are vital and challenging, and the congregation feels that they have a part in them and is challenged by them, then raising the necessary funds becomes personalized and challenging. Raising funds to support "our ministries" is different from raising funds to support "the budget." The same amount of money for the former may be a challenge, for the latter, an impossibility.

Budget Format

There is nothing special about the format you use in presenting your budget to the church. It should be meaningful to them but should not be overly complex. Since the church is familiar with the format of the monthly financial statement[2] you use, you can use the same general format to portray your annual budget for the year (see fig. 2.1). Notice that it shows last year's budget, this year's budget, and the proposal for next year. In addition, you may want to enter the actual "year-to-date" figures while you are preparing your new budget; the actual annual amounts will not be available until you close out your books for the year.

Since your missions program may develop into a multi-faceted program rather quickly, you may want to develop a separate missions budget, a subsidiary to your church budget. Use the same format as your regular church budget so that it will be familiar to the members. In your church budget, show the estimate of the total amount of missions income and expenditures. In your missions budget, you should include more detailed information. Make sure that the amounts shown for missions are the same in both budgets. All you have to do on your missions budget is show how much you expect from each source of missions income and how much you expect to spend for each missions project (see fig. 2.2).

If other special funds are expected to have a great deal of activity during the year, you also may want to develop separate budgets for them as you did for the missions fund. For example, if you are in the construction phase of a building program, you may want to develop a building fund budget. The same rules apply,

Raising funds to support "our ministries" is different from raising funds to support "the budget." The same amount of money for the former may be a challenge, for the latter, an impossibility.

2. Jack A. Henry, *Basic Accounting for Churches* (Nashville, Tenn.: Broadman & Holman, 1994), chap. 9.

	BUDGET—Fiscal Year '95 Church Name Address		
	Budget FY93	Budget FY94	Budget FY95
INCOME			
Regular Offerings	$52,000.00	$56,000.00	$60,000.00
Missions Offerings	10,400.00	11,000.00	15,000.00
Building Fund Offering	5,200.00	5,200.00	7,500.00
Interest on Deposits	400.00	400.00	400.00
Total Income	$68,000.00	$72,600.00	$82,900.00
DISBURSEMENTS			
Staff Salaries	$12,000.00	$14,500.00	$18,000.00
Staff Car Allowance	3,000.00	3,000.00	3,000.00
Staff Housing Allowance	8,000.00	9,000.00	9,000.00
Mortgage Payment	10,800.00	10,800.00	10,800.00
Missions	15,600.00	16,600.00	21,000.00
Utilities	8,400.00	8,500.00	8,600.00
Sunday School Expense	1,200.00	1,200.00	1,200.00
Building Insurance	1,500.00	1,500.00	1,500.00
Building Maintenance	1,000.00	1,000.00	1,000.00
Janitor Supplies	300.00	300.00	300.00
Office Expense	500.00	500.00	500.00
Printing/Advertising	500.00	500.00	500.00
Building Fund Reserve	5,200.00	5,200.00	7,500.00
Total	$68,000.00	$72,600.00	$82,900.00

Figure 2.1 / Church Budget. Notice that 10 percent of the regular offering was spent for missions. Also notice that the total building fund income was held in reserve.

and the same type of budget format can be used for all subsidiary budgets.

Long-Range Plan

After completing the process of developing your annual budget, you will probably find that you have a list of ministries and projects that you really want to do but cannot afford in your budget for this year. Do not throw your list away. Save it and develop a long-term plan for accomplishing those ministries and projects, too.

Missions Budget–Fiscal Year '95
Church Name
Address

	Budget FY93	Budget FY94	Budget FY95
Income:			
Missions Offering	$10,400.00	$11,000.00	$15,000.00
Transfer from General Fund	5,200.00	5,600.00	6,000.00
Total Income	$15,600.00	$16,600.00	$21,000.00
Disbursements:			
Foreign Missions:			
T. Jones	$1,200.00	$1,200.00	$1.800.00
T. Albert	1,200.00	1,200.00	1,800.00
W. Smith	1,200.00	1,200.00	1,800.00
S. Colbert	1,200.00	1,200.00	1,800.00
D. Hankins	1,200.00	1,200.00	1,800.00
T. Milford	600.00	600.00	900.00
Missions Office	300.00	300.00	600.00
Total Foreign Missions	$6,900.00	$6,900.00	$10,500.00
Home Missions:			
Boston	$900.00	$900.00	$1,000.00
Worcester	900.00	900.00	1,000.00
Springfield	900.00	900.00	1,000.00
New Church	300.00	300.00	300.00
Special Project	600.00	600.00	600.00
Total Home Missions	$3,600.00	$3,600.00	$3,900.00
Other:			
Bible College	3,200.00	4,000.00	4,500.00
Missionary Speaker/Hospitality	1,000.00	1,200.00	1,200.00
Missions Conference	900.00	900.00	900.00
Total Other	5,100.00	6,100.00	6,600.00
Total Disbursements	$15,600.00	$16,600.00	$21,000.00

Figure 2.2 / Missions Budget. This budget is subsidiary to the church budget shown in fig. 2.1. Notice that the total missions offering and disbursements are the same for missions in both budgets.

Five years is often used as the basis for long-term plans; however, they can be three-year plans or ten-year plans, depending on what you decide is best for your church. The plan does not have to be complicated, but it should be written. You should include estimates for income as well as for expenses, and you should briefly describe the basis for making your estimates. Remember, making estimates of income and expenses for one year is hard work and an inexact science, so making estimates several years into the future is even more inexact.

Begin your plan by assigning priorities to all of the ministries, projects, capital purchases, and other things you want to do but could not include in this year's budget. Based on the priorities you assigned, decide on what year in the future you think you will be able to include them in your budget and write the year next to the project. Then, arrange the list according to the year you plan to add them to the budget.

Using the same format shown in figure 2.1, start with the year beyond the new budget year and include headings for the number of years you decided to include in your long-range plan. Consider each income and expense category and establish the rationale for its increase or decrease for each year. You may want to estimate some added income due to church growth or added expenses due to inflation, etc. As you consider each year and each line item for that year, use the list of leftover projects and ministries as reminders to specifically include them in your estimate.

Figure 2.3 illustrates a long-range plan using five years as the basis for planning and the information in figure 2.1 as the starting point. It assumes church growth, which results in growth in income as well as an increase in expenses. It also assumes that some of your "leftover" unfunded goals for the current budget year include adding some part-time staff, increasing the pastor's salary package each year to cover inflation (plus some additional amount to recognize his good ministry), expanding your Sunday School ministries, and establishing a contingency fund and building it to the point where it contains one month's general fund income.

The resulting five-year plan is used each year when beginning work on your new budget. The appropriate year is lifted directly out of the five-year plan to be the basis for developing your new budget. When using a long-term plan such as this, remember two things: (1) the estimates used in the long-term plan will not be as accurate as you can make them now by using the current information you have in your church bookkeeping system, and (2) you will need to add another year onto the end of your five-year plan to keep it projected five years into the future.

Summary

Budgeting is a process, not an action. You must set goals and priorities as well as make estimates of income and expenses—all of it is hard work.

You must know your congregation and have open lines of communication with them so that you will have their input in the goal and priority-setting process. Consideration of every potential ministry of the church is essential if you are to develop a budget that truly reflects the utmost in ministry for the church. When all goals and priorities are processed through the sieve of reflection and prayer, you can be sure your budget will be helpful in the work of the ministry.

You can never be exact in your estimates, either for income or expenses. But your estimates are better than nothing and will help you make adjustments as your budget year progresses. Your bookkeeping records are your best sources of information for making estimates, but remember that they are history and not prophecy—you still have to use your best judgment when developing your budget.

Balancing your budget is "crunch time." No matter how tempting it might be to "juggle the numbers a little" at this point, it will not help. To finalize a budget that is meaningful and useable, you have to make those final decisions that select the most important minis-

		FIVE YEAR PLAN Church Name Address			
	FY96	**FY97**	**FY98**	**FY99**	**FY00**
INCOME:					
Regular Offerings	$65,000.00	$71,000.00	$78,000.00	$85,000.00	$93,000.00
Missions Offerings	16,000.00	17,000.00	18,000.00	21,000.00	23,000.00
Building Fund Offering	6,500.00	7,100.00	7,800.00	8,500.00	9,300.00
Interest on Deposits	500.00	600.00	600.00	600.00	650.00
Total Income	$88,000.00	$95,700.00	$104,400.00	$115,100.00	$125,950.00
DISBURSEMENTS:					
Staff Salaries	$19,500.00	$19,500.00	$20,000.00	$24,400.00	$28,000.00
Staff Car Expense	4,000.00	4,000.00	4,500.00	4,500.00	5,500.00
Staff Housing Allowance	9,000.00	10,000.00	11,000.00	12,000.00	13,000.00
Staff Health Insurance	0.00	4,000.00	4,000.00	4,000.00	4,000.00
Mortgage Payment	10,800.00	10,800.00	10,800.00	10,800.00	10,800.00
Missions	22,500.00	24,100.00	25,800.00	29,500.00	32,300.00
Utilities	8,800.00	9,000.00	9,200.00	9,400.00	9,600.00
Sunday School Expense	2,000.00	2,000.00	2,400.00	2,400.00	2,400.00
Building Insur- ance	1,800.00	1,900.00	2,000.00	2,100.00	2,500.00
Building Mainte- nance	1,500.00	1,500.00	2,400.00	1,800.00	2,400.00
Janitor Supplies	400.00	600.00	1,000.00	900.00	900.00
Office Expense	700.00	600.00	600.00	900.00	900.00
Printing/ Advertising	500.00	600.00	900.00	900.00	1,200.00
Contingency Reserve	0.00	0.00	2,000.00	3,000.00	3,150.00
Building Fund Reserve	6,500.00	7,100.00	7,800.00	8,500.00	9,300.00
Total	$88,000.00	$95,700.00	$104,400.00	$115,100.00	$125,950.00

Figure 2.3/ Five-Year Plan. A long-range plan such as this can be developed for any length of time you decide to use. Five years was used only for the purpose of illustration. The format is the same regardless of the length of time used.

tries for your church for the budget year and set aside the others for other times and other circumstances.

When you don't include a particular ministry in your budget, you are not making a statement about whether it is good or bad. You are only saying that for this year, in this church, the ministries that you did include will be the best use of the resources God has given you at this time. The others that you wish to pursue should become part of your long-range plan.

Just as everything you do regarding church finances should be simple, keep your budget format simple too.

Your bookkeeping records . . . are history and not prophecy— you still have to use your best judgment when developing your budget.

Chapter 3

I have planted, Apollos watered; but God gave the in-crease.

So then neither is he that planteth any thing, neither he that watereth; but God that giveth the increase.

Now he that planteth and he that watereth are one: and every man shall receive his own reward according to his own labour.

For we are labourers together with God: ye are God's husbandry, ye are God's building.

—1 Corinthians 3:6–9

The Budget Approval Process

The budget is a guide for the entire church, not just for the pastor or finance committee. Every church member should be engaged in ministry work in some way, so every member is affected by the budget.

Realistically, we know that not everybody gets involved in church ministries, but nearly everyone wants to have an opportunity to "have a say" in how the church's money is spent. Because church members are affected by the budget, they should be involved in the budget development and approval process to the maximum extent possible.

The budget process gives the pastor an opportunity to teach the whole church about the needs of the church and the importance of each ministry he is

> The budget is a guide for the entire church, not just for the pastor or finance committee.

thinking about funding. It can sometimes be the stimulus to cause nonworkers to get involved. Deacons, trustees, the finance committee, and ministry leaders constitute small working groups who are knowledgeable about the needs and opportunities of the church's various ministries. However, because of their work on the budget, they, too, may become more interested in their own ministry areas, expand their personal horizons into new ministries, or become active recruiters of new volunteers. Helping to develop the budget may give them a new insight into the magnitude of the task or the opportunities of the moment.

The pastor's vision for the ministry of the church for the coming year is the key element for developing the church budget, regardless of the size of the church. The pastor knows what the ministry challenges and opportunities are, he knows what his resources are—both personnel and financial resources—and he knows what the costs have been in the past and are likely to be in the future. In short, a pastor who has really assumed his biblical role as leader and shepherd of the flock is a one-man budget committee in a small church, especially one that is newly established. He must remain the final decision maker in a church of any size because he is responsible for its spiritual leadership, and budget priorities directly reflect the church's spiritual priorities.

When making plans for the first budget of a new baby church, there is not much of an approval process. If the mission church has close ties with a sponsoring church that is in the same area and is able to provide close supervision and guidance, then the budget development process may be directed or controlled by the sponsoring church. When the new mission church is not nearby, however, the pastor and his family may be the only ones present that first Sunday, and approving a budget for the new church may merely mean approving one that suits the pastor. Do not fall into the trap, however, of not having a written budget even if there is only one person involved. Remember, a budget helps guide your actions and frees you from having to make

The pastor's vision for the ministry of the church for the coming year is the key element for developing the church budget.

a myriad of minor daily decisions. It also provides you with a basis for checking on how you are doing in relation to your plans. A budget is necessary even for a congregation just getting started—even if the approval process involves merely a one-man decision.

The Budget Committee

The size of the budget committee should be kept small so that it can be flexible in operation and still perform its duties effectively. The composition of the budget committee is often spelled out in the church constitution or bylaws and often consists of the deacons or trustees, or both, depending on how the church is organized. The church treasurer should be on the committee, but church bylaws sometimes overlook this obvious member. Many times church bylaws establish a finance committee instead of a budget committee. When this happens, the finance committee is usually given responsibility for budget-related duties. In any event, be sure to follow your church's written procedures regarding membership of the committee. Make formal changes to the procedures whenever it is necessary.

The size of the budget committee should be kept small so that it can be flexible in operation and still perform its duties effectively.

If the pastor is allowed some discretion in selecting members for the budget committee, he should give more weight to ministry experience than to financial management experience. A person who is actively involved in another ministry of the church is much more apt to understand the spiritual nature of the budget decisions that must be made than someone who merely has the professional skills to work with financial data. The person who is already involved with the church's ministries is much more willing to pray for the Lord's leadership and follow His will when it becomes clear than one who has not had that experience.

In selecting members for the budget committee, . . . give more weight to ministry experience than to financial management experience.

Those not active in ministry may see only money problems and remain untouched by spiritual opportunities. On the other hand, do not overlook people just because they have professional financial management skills. These professionals may also include some of your best workers in some of your ministries. The main point is that the work of the church involves walking by faith, and those who are experiencing that walk now will be the best qualified to lead into the future.

Time Factors

The length of time it takes to develop and approve a budget depends on the size of the congregation and the complexity of its organization. The larger the departments are in your church, the longer it takes for them to develop departmental budgets to be included in the overall church budget. The more departments you have, the more time it takes to coordinate with each of them and to insure that their requests are complete and justified. And finally, the more departments you have and the larger they are, the harder it is to gain consensus about the priority of each ministry, project, or function that is to be included in the budget.

The overall time it takes to prepare a church budget can vary from a few days for a "baby church" to several months for a large congregation. Plan to have time for your people to think and pray as well as to meet and "figure." Allow time for research to be done, if necessary, and for coordination between working groups. If your budget process extends over a period of several months, you may have to cancel at least one meeting because of sickness or other personal emergency of one or more key workers. After planning for all of these allowances, make sure you do not spread the process out too long, or your workers may not feel any sense of urgency about completing the task.

Plan to have time for your people to think and pray as well as to meet and "figure."

Small Church

There is no key number of members or attendance that makes a church "large" or "small." The key element is the size and complexity of the organization. For the sake of discussion, the term "small church" is used to mean a church that is not departmentalized in its Sunday School or other ministries. It may have Sunday School classes for all ages, bus ministries, music ministries, etc., but all of the leaders of the individual ministries are directly responsible to the pastor rather than to a departmental superintendent or other leader.

Although the pastor is the key figure in developing a small church's budget, he should not be the only figure unless the church is a newly formed congregation with no other workers involved in its ministry. If the church has grown beyond that point, others who are engaged in the church's ministries should be included at some point. The prayerful input of all available mature Christians is imperative. Also, by including teachers and other ministry leaders in the development of the budget, support for the budget is gained while it is being developed.

Beginning the Process

The pastor of a small church with few workers should develop a complete budget by himself before involving the workers. This budget is only tentative until it is approved by the church, but it will require very few changes before being approved if it has been well thought out. If the church is still so new that it is not yet formally organized as a church, this budget may not even need to be formally approved. However, the information in it should be shared with those who intend to be members when the church is formally organized.

In developing the church budget, the pastor should follow the procedures outlined in chapter 2: set goals, establish priorities, estimate income and expenses, and "balance the budget." He should then review the current year's budget and actual results and compare these figures with his plan for the upcoming year. This comparison will make any omissions immediately obvious. It will also highlight new sources of income or expense so that they can be discussed with the congregation.

Advantages of Involving People

1. ***Creates Ownership.*** The budget becomes "their budget," not the preacher's budget or the church's budget.
2. ***Educates Members.*** Members participating in the budget development become aware of the church's goals and priorities.
3. ***Reduces Late Changes.*** All relevant input is included in early stages of budget development.
4. ***"Sells" the Budget Ahead of Time.*** All pertinent questions are answered during budget development instead of at the time for approval.
5. ***Protects Pastor's Reputation.*** Precludes charges of dictatorial leadership.

---

1 to 4 Weeks for Approval

The time from start to finish for the development of a small church's budget depends on the time it takes for the pastor to develop his personal plan for the church. Time for coordination with workers can often be done in one meeting, and approval by the church does not require long lead time to ensure that everybody is informed. From start to finish, the budget process in a small church might be as short as one week but often takes two to four weeks. Be sure to start far enough in advance so the process is not hurried.

Be sure to start far enough in advance so the [budget] process is not hurried.

Large Church

Beginning the Process

Although there are many people involved in developing a budget for a large church, the core of the budget should emanate from the heart of the pastor. He has been called of God to lead the church spiritually. The budget is merely a plan that attaches dollars and cents to the outward workings—the ministry applications—of that spiritual leadership.

The apostle Peter advised pastors to lead by example, but he also exhorted them to take the oversight of the flock (1 Pet. 5:2–3). Sometimes pastors are tempted to abdicate their responsibility to lead in financial matters and leave it to the church members to decide how to allocate and spend church funds. This temptation may be especially strong if the church by-laws place the authority to control church funds in the hands of one or more committees. The temptation is fortified even more if a strong-willed or outspoken member always opposes the pastor. No matter what the circumstances, however, the budget reflects the spiritual direction the congregation is planning to take for the coming year, and the pastor must play the leading role in steering the course.

> The budget reflects the spiritual direction the congregation is planning to take for the coming year, and the pastor must play the leading role in steering the course.

3 to 6 Months Before Final Approval

In a large congregation with many large departments, the budget process should begin three to six months before the date it is to be approved. The beginning of the annual process may be a sermon by the pastor on a Sunday morning that lays out a challenge for the upcoming year and expresses thanksgiving for the blessings on this year's ministry. At this time, a date is set for the first meeting of the finance committee, department heads, and other appropriate leaders of the congregation to begin work on the new budget.

When the pastor announces the initial meeting of the workers involved in developing the budget, he can solicit input from the entire congregation. He can do this by introducing the people who will be developing the budget so everybody in the congregation will know who to go to with their suggestions. People do not always want to take part in the budget process, but they always want to feel like they are included in it.

> People do not always want to take part in the budget process, but they always want to feel like they are included in it.

The First Budget Committee Meeting. Before meeting with all workers who are going to be involved with the budget preparation process, the pastor should meet with just the budget committee. This meeting could be conducted on the same evening as the meeting of all workers if the meetings are focused and short.

The pastor should know in advance who can best handle each position on the budget committee and should have discussed the assignments with the individuals concerned before the meeting to gain their acceptance. At the meeting he makes the appointments and outlines each committee member's duties and responsibilities. By doing this, everybody will know who is responsible for each portion of the budget or budget process, and no time will be wasted in begging or coercing people to accept assignments. Nothing can be more time consuming and boring than listening to someone who is obviously qualified make his humble apologies for his inadequacy so the leader can point out all of his qualifications for everyone to behold.

After each committee member accepts his or her assignment, target dates for completing each step of the budget preparation process should be agreed on. From this point on, every budget committee member should have a job, know what is expected of him or her, and know when the job should be finished.

The First Budget Meeting. Although the size of the budget committee should be kept small so that members can work together easily, the leaders of every church ministry should be invited to an initial meeting with the pastor and the budget committee. The pastor should lead the meeting and ensure that all participants recognize the spiritual character of the entire process. At this meeting he should share his vision for the direction and progress of the church for the coming year in more specific terms than in his original challenge to the church. He should also indicate why new directions and new ministries may be possible or needed for the coming year.

The pastor uses this first meeting of all of the ministry leaders to teach them how to develop their part of the budget. Leaders who have been through the process before usually need a refresher, and those who

> The leaders of every church ministry should be invited to an initial meeting with the pastor and the budget committee.

have not need to know exactly what is expected of them.

When you have explained what information is needed from them and why, and have demonstrated how to complete the budget forms (see fig. 3.1) and where to turn them in, remember to tell the leaders when you want the information—set deadlines and secure their acceptance by every leader. It is important that you have the information from all of the departments and ministries at the time agreed on so your budget committee can consolidate, review, validate, and coordinate preliminary changes before they begin to prayerfully consider the final budget package.

The more departments or ministries you have preparing budget requests, the longer this collection process will take. Most of your workers will not understand the need for a long lead time before the budget is presented to the church unless you explain it to them—so do not forget to explain it. Your workers will be a lot more conscientious about meeting the established deadlines if they understand their importance.

Making Budget Requests. If you have simple and specific guidance for your workers, they will usually try hard to follow it and will feel a sense of accomplishment when they have successfully done what has been asked of them. A budget request form can be very useful in keeping the budget process simple (see fig. 3.1). As you can see, not only can you get the "what" and "how much" information you want, but you can even get an idea of when an expenditure will need to be made—all from a simple form.

If any budget items are going to be consolidated, decide on whether you want each department to order enough of the item to meet their needs or if someone else is going to take care of ordering for the entire church. For example, your Sunday School superintendent, head usher, and church secretary can decide on how many offering envelopes and other administrative supplies will be needed for the church without trying to get every departmental leader into the act of making

Remember to tell the leaders when you want the information—set deadlines and secure their acceptance by every leader.

BUDGET REQUEST FOR F Y '94

Department _Teens_   Preparer _Bill Jones_

Date _10/15/93_

PART 1. Use one form for each line item requested. Be as accurate as possible when estimating costs. Use the remarks section to explain why you need the item, and how you arrived at your cost estimate.

If you have a special reason for an item to be purchased at a special place, give the reason in the reason in remarks and show the special place as the "Source."

DESCRIPTION: _Youth Chorus Books_

SOURCE: _____

TOTAL COST: _$250.00_

REMARKS: _50 books @5.00 each. Books are needed for teen activities + for Sunday School. Half are needed now + balance for summer activities._

PART 2. After determining the total cost for the year, show how much of the total amount you want to spend each month for this line item.

January: $ _125.00_   July: $ _____

February: $ _____   August: $ _____

March: $ _____   September: $ _____

April: $ _____   October: $ _____

May: $ _125.00_   September: $ _____

June: $ _____   December: $ _____

Figure 3.1/ Sample Budget Request Form. This is the basic form used by leaders of each area of ministry to submit their request for items t—hat are to be included in the next year's budget.

estimates for their departments. Do not get too bogged down in detail. Eliminate all of the paperwork you can from your ministry leaders and let them spend their time on their ministries.

On the other hand, if you are going to purchase replacement audio-visual materials for the Sunday School, the departmental leaders will need to check with each teacher to determine individual needs before they can establish the needs for their departments. In that case, you would want each department to request the amount needed for replacement materials in their own department. You would consolidate all the requests later for the total church budget.

No matter how conscientious you feel your workers are, you need to follow up on their progress to insure they meet the agreed-on deadlines. Follow-up actions can be viewed by workers as being "nosey" unless you establish the proper working relationship with them. Use your follow-up contacts to be helpful. Answer questions, suggest sources of information your workers may not be aware of, help them coordinate with other committees when necessary, and encourage their suggestions. This can be one of the most rewarding functions of your ministry if it helps you and your congregational leaders become better acquainted so you can minister together better as a team.

> Follow-up actions can be viewed by workers as being "nosey" unless you establish the proper working relationship with them.

2 to 3 Months Before Final Approval

By this time, departmental budgets should be in the hands of the budget committee. It is during this time period that departmental budget requests are consolidated and budget balancing decisions are made. Initially, all of the requests are consolidated by the budget committee without making any adjustments.

The income estimates for each fund category, i.e., general, missions, building, etc., are also computed during this time. These income estimates are usually made by either the pastor or the church's business manager because they have the best grasp of the causes for variances in this year's estimates. If the pastor does not make the income estimates, he must tell the one who does about any special fund drives he is planning for the year. If expected income warrants it, you could give everybody everything they want—unfortunately it seldom happens that way.

After consolidating all of the requests, check the combined list to make sure you have not overlooked any ministry, department, project, or other expense category. When certain that the draft budget is complete, go over the justification for each item of expense to satisfy yourself that each item is legitimately needed. You are now ready to begin the process of balancing the budget—of getting the expenses equal to or less than the income.

> After consolidating all of the requests, check the combined list to make sure you have not overlooked any ministry, department, project, or other expense category.

It is at this point that you will use the priorities you established at the beginning of the budget process to help you make decisions. One department may request funds for a project they would "like to do" as well as for things that are essential if they are to be effective. If the department's ministry is one of your high priorities, you may automatically approve the essentials, but delay final approval of the request for non-essential funds until you have considered the requests of all other departments and ministries.

After evaluating all of the budget requests, you may decide to eliminate a project or ministry to give the high-priority department the extra funds requested, or you may decide to keep all of the departments and ministries and deny the extra funds requested by the high priority department. Either way, priorities you established at the beginning of the budget process to guide the ministry of your church for the coming year will be the determining factors in how to spend your available funds.

When you have completed your first draft of a complete, balanced budget, arrange a meeting with each department or ministry leader whose budget request was substantially changed. You will want that leader to understand why you did not fund his budget request. It may be that you like the idea but must delay funding it because of other priorities; it may be that you like the idea so well that you want to build it into a larger project for the entire church and need more time to develop it; or it may be that the idea does not fit into the ministry plans for the church. If the reason for not funding is one of the former, then he is encouraged and can probably be counted on to help you develop the idea for later use. If it is because it does not fit the church's plans for ministry, he needs to know it so he does not cause future misunderstandings by promoting a program that the pastor and church lay leadership have already decided against.

1 to 2 Months Before Final Approval

After reviewing, revising, and trimming the budget numbers—and a great deal of prayer—you arrive at a

> Priorities you established at the beginning of the budget process to guide the ministry of your church for the coming year will be the determining factors in how to spend your available funds.

> Arrange a meeting with each department or ministry leader whose budget request was substantially changed. You will want that leader to understand why you did not fund his budget request.

final draft of your proposed budget for the new year. When the pastor and budget committee have approved it, it is time to present this final draft budget to the entire deacon or trustee board for approval if that is required by your by-laws. It is also time to call another meeting of all the department and ministry leaders to answer any final questions they may have and gain their support.

The pastor should lead this meeting and show how this budget is going to translate into spiritual ministries and blessings for the coming year. The meeting should be very positive and should not take long because the important or "sticky" questions will have already been answered during the process of budget development.

If there were new programs or ministries suggested during the budget process that were not included in the budget but should be considered for the future, the pastor can tell about them and secure active prayer support for their development. These ideas for potential future ministries are positive results of the budget process that are not reflected in the budget itself. Pointing out these indirect benefits of the budget process, benefits that are actually spiritual in nature, can help transform the dreary work of budgeting into an exciting experience with spiritual expectations.

> Ideas for potential future ministries are positive results of the budget process that are not reflected in the budget itself.

Final Month Before Approval

Each church member needs to feel that the budget he will be asked to approve is "his budget." That can only be done if each member has had time to read it, pray about it, and get his questions about it answered. Therefore, after being approved by all of the ministry leaders, the proposed budget should be printed and prepared for distribution. Do not print all of the justifications or explanations, etc.; just print the numbers in the format suggested in fig 2.1. If there are subsidiary budgets, such as a missions budget, be sure that they are included.

The size of a church will affect how the proposed budget is distributed. A good start would be to post a copy of it on the church bulletin board and call attention to it. In addition, print enough copies so it can be distributed at either the Sunday evening service or mid-week prayer service. The pastor should again introduce the members of the budget committee and tell of their availability to answer questions about the budget. During this entire process, emphasize that the budget is the result of the coordinated work and prayer of every ministry leader in the church over an extended period of time. Also, be sure to announce when they will be asked to vote on its approval.

When announcing the meeting to vote on the budget, do not take questions. Make it known that every ministry leader is recommending it, the budget committee is recommending it, and the pastor is recommending it. With those recommendations and the knowledge that their questions can be answered privately by one of the budget committee members, there will be a general awareness of the openness of the entire process and a ready acceptance of its outcome, the budget.

> Emphasize the fact that the budget is the result of the coordinated work and prayer of every ministry leader in the church over an extended period of time.

The Meeting to Approve the Budget

Some pastors and churches dread the business meeting when the budget is to be adopted; but if proper preparations are made, this meeting should be one of the spiritual highlights of the church year.

The pastor should conduct the meeting, and the members of the budget committee should be on the platform with him. Extra copies of the budget should be available for handing out to members who have not previously received a copy, and a visual aid such as a chalkboard or an overhead projector should be used so the entire congregation can view the budget as it is being presented.

A typical church business meeting for approving the annual budget starts with prayer. The pastor then reviews the process by which the budget was developed and approved up to this point. He should emphasize that it started with prayerful consideration of the church's mission and ministry and that it reflects the

> If proper preparations are made, the meeting held to approve the budget should be one of the spiritual highlights of the church year.

church's spiritual goals for the coming year. Time may also be taken to briefly summarize highlights of some of the victories in the high-priority ministries during the current year, the goals for those ministries for the next year, and how this proposed budget will support the achievement of those goals. If new ministries have been added or substantial changes have been made to old ones, be sure to give a brief explanation about why making those adjustments will help the church better achieve its overall goals.

The pastor should also explain that the approval being requested is to use the budget being presented as a guide. He should explain and illustrate how some amounts might be changed with the approval of the pastor or business manager, larger amounts will be changed only after approval of the deacons or finance commitee, and even larger changes will be made only with the approval of the entire church. He should remind them that even small variations will be reported in the monthly financial statements which are posted for all members to review.

When the pastor completes his presentation, he should re-emphasize that the deacon/trustee board, the budget committee, and the leaders of every ministry of the church are recommending approval of this proposed budget. He should then ask if there are any questions and give direct answers to any that are asked.

Do not expect questions, and do not try to "pump" them out of the congregation. If the pastor and his co-workers have done a good job of developing the budget and presenting it to the congregation, it will be obvious to everyone that it should be approved. Do not spark controversy—do strive for unity. Do not prolong the meeting—do ask for the vote. After pausing briefly to allow questions, lead in prayer and vote.

Do not spark controversy—do strive for unity. Do not prolong the meeting—do ask for the vote. After pausing briefly to allow questions, lead in prayer and vote.

Summary and Conclusion

Developing and approving the budget is a process, not an act. The process requires the pastor and other leaders in the church to review the mission and each of

The final budget is a direct reflection of the plans for the church's spiritual direction.

the ministries of the church, their goals and achievements, and, based on their evaluation, to lead the congregation into the coming year. The entire process relies heavily upon spiritual leadership because the entire purpose of the budget is to provide for the spiritual ministries of the church. The final budget is a direct reflection of the plans for the church's spiritual direction.

As workers at all levels think about their own ministries and needs for the coming year, they gain a better grasp of their personal goals and a better understanding of how their department, or ministry, fits into the overall church program. While discussing ministry goals and needs, leaders at all levels have the opportunity to enlist non-committed members into the active ministry of the church.

A united congregation is a major, collateral outcome of a well-thought-out, prayerfully developed, complete and challenging budget.

Chapter 4

When thou vowest a vow unto God, defer not to pay it; for
he hath no pleasure in fools: pay that which thou hast vowed.
Better is it that thou shouldest not vow, than that thou
shouldest vow and not pay.

—*Ecclesiastes 5:4–5*

Cash Flow Budgets

In this world of credit cards, mortgages, charge accounts, and delayed payment plans, it is common for
individuals to accumulate more debt than they can pay
for on a timely basis. Many large, stable, old-line businesses have been forced into bankruptcy proceedings
because they did not have enough cash on hand to pay
their bills on time. They may have owned buildings,
land, and equipment worth much more than they
owed, or large amounts of money may have been owed
to them. However, these businesses could not pay their
bills because they did not have the cash flow to provide
the cash needed at the time they needed it.

God tells Christians to "provide things honest in the
sight of all men" (Rom. 12:17), and He expects His
children to do just that. Not only does God expect it of
Christians, but the world does too. They especially expect it of churches. Businessmen expect churches to

pay bills on time even though they may not hold the general public to the same high standard.

A Word of Caution

Your annual church budget shows planned income and expenses for the year. It may be in balance or even have a substantial planned surplus. However, if large expenditures are made during the early part of the year and income only increases gradually during the course of the year, cash flow may not be sufficient to allow you to pay your bills when they are due. You may find yourself paying bills late and bringing reproach on God and your church if you do not plan the timing of your income and expenses as well as planning their total amounts.

The cash flow budget for a church is nothing more than the annual budget broken into shorter time increments. By breaking your budget into shorter time increments, you can plan the timing of your spending to coincide with the expected timing of your income. You can keep from making major purchases during times when you expect income to be low; and you can identify times when larger than usual bank balances do not represent unexpected spending opportunities, but are there to pay for planned expenses that have not yet occurred. Large bank balances that are needed to pay for budgeted needs must not be spent "by mistake" for unplanned items, even if those items are useful for the church's ministry.

An Update

A cash flow budget also helps you evaluate how you are doing in relation to the annual budget. By comparing your monthly financial statement—what actually happened—with your cash flow budget for the same month, you have a "progress report" as you go through your budget year. You do not have to wait until the end of the year to see how you are doing. This timely comparison helps determine if budget adjustments are

You may find yourself paying bills late and bringing reproach on God and your church if you do not plan the timing of your income and expenses as well as planning their total amounts.

The cash flow budget for a church is nothing more than the annual budget broken into shorter time increments.

needed and may even give you an indication of what adjustments to make.

A cash flow budget also helps you evaluate how you are doing in relation to the annual budget.

All of the benefits derived from developing and using a cash flow budget for the church's general fund also apply to subsidiary budgets the church may have. Procedures for developing subsidiary cash flow budgets are the same as those discussed below for the church's general fund. Figure 4.3 illustrates a cash flow budget for the missions budget which is a subsidiary budget.

Developing a Cash Flow Budget

A month is a good time frame for a cash flow budget. Most expenses come in monthly increments—the phone and utility bills, open account purchases, etc.— so it is easy to plan for them on a monthly basis. Churches may try to apportion weekly offerings into each budget category, but that usually proves to be too cumbersome and does not really add to the control you have by using the month as your time frame. The monthly amount needed for expense items paid weekly, such as payroll or a sinking fund payment, can be easily computed by counting the number of weeks in each month.

A month is a good time frame for a cash flow budget.

If you used a form similar to the budget request form in figure 3.1 when you developed your annual budget, you already have a good idea about the desired timing of expenditures. If you also used the form in developing your income estimates, you have a good idea of the amount of income you can expect each month. If you have this information available from your budget development process, then developing a preliminary cash flow budget requires nothing more than mechanically making twelve monthly budgets based on the estimates and desires already recorded. Notice that the total of the twelve "monthly budgets" in figure 4.1 is the same as the amount shown for the same item in the Budget FY94 column in figure 2.1 except for missions. The $11,000 of offerings designated for missions were deposited directly into the missions fund. The amount shown for missions in figure 4.1 is the 10 percent of the regular offering that is transferred to the missions fund each month. Notice that the missions cash flow budget, figure 4.3, includes both the designated offerings and the amount that is transferred from the general fund

Although a cash flow budget is essentially a group of twelve monthly budgets, you cannot just divide the numbers in your annual budget by twelve to arrive at a monthly cash flow budget. Neither your income nor your expenses are the same each month. Often, your income is above average in the spring and fall and below average in the summer and winter. If you plan for an increase in income, it will probably occur gradually throughout the year, as your congregation grows, instead of in twelve equal increments. Your expenses for heating are high in the winter and low in the summer— air conditioning expenses are the reverse. If you plan pay raises to begin at some time other than the first of the budget year or if you plan to hire staff during the course of the year, then the payroll will change accordingly. There is no shortcut. You must evaluate every budget item and apportion it on a monthly basis throughout the year according to your best estimate.

If your church has been in existence more than a year, your monthly financial statements for the past year should be compared to this preliminary cash flow budget. This will show if any obvious major differences in the timing of expected income or expenditures exist between what was requested and your experience from last year. If there are differences, you can evaluate them and decide which should be chosen for the new budget year. Keep in mind that there may be good reasons for differences: you may have changed the month for your missions conference, so the increase in missions giving would begin at a different month; or you may have changed the month for youth camp, so the youth department budget will need money for camp related expenses at a different time. All obvious differences between requests for next year and the experience of this year should be noted and evaluated, and a decision

You must evaluate every budget item and apportion it on a monthly basis throughout the year according to your best estimate.

If your church has been in existence more than a year, your monthly financial statements for the past year should be compared to this preliminary cash flow budget.

GENERAL FUND CASH FLOW—Fiscal Year '9___
Church Name
Address

	JAN	FEB	MAR	APR	MAY	JUN	JUL	AUG	SEP	OCT	NOV	DEC	TOTAL
INCOME:													
Reg Offer.	4000	4000	4000	4500	4500	4500	4500	4500	5000	6000	5500	5000	56000
Interest	30	30	30	40	35	40	35	30	30	35	35	30	400
Total	4030	4030	4030	4540	4535	4540	4535	4530	5030	6035	5535	5030	56400
DISBURSEMENTS:													
Staff Salaries	1000	1000	1250	1000	1000	1000	1000	1250	1500	1500	1500	1500	14500
Staff Car Exp.	250	200	250	250	250	200	250	250	300	300	250	250	3000
Staff Housing	750	750	750	750	750	750	750	750	750	750	750	750	9000
Mortgage Pmnt.	900	900	900	900	900	900	900	900	900	900	900	900	10800
Miss-Transfer	400	400	400	450	450	450	450	450	500	600	550	500	5600
Utilities	900	900	800	850	500	500	700	800	500	500	750	800	8500
Sunday School	50	50	150	50	50	50	300	250	50	50	100	50	1200
Building Ins.	0	375	0	0	375	0	0	375	0	0	375	0	1500
Building Maint.	100	50	50	100	50	150	150	100	50	50	50	100	1000
Janitor Sup.	25	50	50	0	50	25	50	25	25	0	25	25	300
Office Expense	50	50	50	25	25	25	50	25	50	50	50	50	500
Print/Adv.	0	0	0	100	0	100	200	0	0	0	100	0	500
Total	4425	4675	4650	4475	4400	4150	4800	5175	4625	4700	5400	4925	56400
Monthly Tot.	-395	-645	-620	+65	+135	+390	-265	-645	+405	+1335	+135	+105	0

Figure 4.1/ Cash Flow Budget. This shows a year's annual budget divided into monthly divisions. It shows when budget items are expected to be purchased and which months are projected to have surpluses or deficits.

made about which one to use in determining the final cash flow budget for the new year

From this preliminary cash flow budget, you can determine if there will be enough money each month throughout the year to pay the expected bills when they are due. In figure 4.1, one additional line of information, Monthly Total, has been added to show you at a glance if there will be a surplus or deficit each month. You can also use this line to compute your expected bank balance at any point in the new budget year, providing your cash flow assumptions are correct. By starting with the anticipated cash balance in the bank at the end of the previous year and adding or subtracting the monthly surplus or deficit shown on this added line, you can easily compute what your bank balance will be at the end of each month. This expected bank balance is computed just like computing a "balance forward" in your checkbook.

Instead of estimating your checkbook balance for each month while you are developing the budget, you may want to see only what the greatest amount of surplus or deficit will be during the budget year. Figure 4.2 has a second line of information added to show the expected *cumulative* cash flow at the end of each month. Each month's surplus or deficit is added to the cumulative surplus or deficit of the previous month. Instead of computing estimated monthly bank balances to help you decide if spending adjustments are needed, you may prefer to use this cumulative surplus/deficit information. If the largest cumulative deficit expected for any month during the new budget year is less than the bank balance you expect to end the current year with, you will have enough money to cover your largest deficit expected during the new budget year. If the largest cumulative deficit is more than your expected ending bank balance for the current year, then you will have to reschedule some of your spending to be able to pay all of your bills on time.

By estimating cash balances, you can decide how to change the timing of the income or expenses so sufficient cash will be available when it is needed. After all of the adjustments are made to coordinate the expected income with the expected expenses, you will have a cash flow budget that can be used to help manage the church's cash assets to ensure that the bills are paid on time.

You can also see from figure 4.2 that your plan results in a cumulative deficit every month during the year, except the last when income finally catches up with spending. Even if the last fiscal year ends with $1,000 in the bank, the church will become delinquent in paying bills as early as February because the cumulative deficit is more than $1,000. Your plan's largest total deficit will occur during August when the month ends with $1,980 less than you had when you started the year. If you planned to end the previous year with a surplus, you can tell from looking at these monthly cumulative deficits which month's cash flow plans need to be changed, and how much to change them, to be able to pay your bills on time.

You might wish to add the cumulative total line to your missions cash flow budget too. If you did, you would see that your missions fund would be short $25 in January, $375 in May, $675 in July, and $1,000 in October, even though you would come out even at the end of the year. If your income estimates are valid, then you must either change the timing of some missions expenditures; borrow money from the general fund, if there is money available; or develop a plan to secure additional income. If you do nothing, you will not be able to keep your promises to your missionaries.

Using the Cash Flow Budget

The cash flow budget helps you make spending decisions because it gives you a picture of your expected cash assets at any point in time. It shows you when large or unusual expenditures are planned and make it possible to compute whether there will be enough cash to cover those expenditures.

For example, if your church must make a large expenditure at a specific time and the cash flow budget

GENERAL FUND CASH FLOW—Fiscal Year '9__
Church Name
Address

	JAN	FEB	MAR	APR	MAY	JUN	JUL	AUG	SEP	OCT	NOV	DEC	TOTAL
INCOME:													
Reg Offer.	4000	4000	4000	4500	4500	4500	4500	4500	5000	6000	5500	5000	56000
Interest	30	30	30	40	35	40	35	30	30	35	35	30	400
Total	4030	4030	4030	4540	4535	4540	4535	4530	5030	6035	5535	5030	56400
DISBURSEMENTS:													
Staff Salaries	1000	1000	1250	1000	1000	1000	1000	1250	1500	1500	1500	1500	14500
Staff Car Exp.	250	200	250	250	250	200	250	250	300	300	250	250	3000
Staff Housing	750	750	750	750	750	750	750	750	750	750	750	750	9000
Mortgage Pmnt.	900	900	900	900	900	900	900	900	900	900	900	900	10800
Miss-Transfer	400	400	400	450	450	450	450	450	500	600	550	500	5600
Utilities	900	900	800	850	500	500	700	800	500	500	750	800	8500
Sunday School	50	50	150	50	50	50	300	250	50	50	100	50	1200
Building Ins.	0	375	0	0	375	0	0	375	0	0	375	0	1500
Building Maint.	100	50	50	100	50	150	150	100	50	50	50	100	1000
Janitor Sup.	25	0	50	0	50	25	50	25	25	0	25	25	300
Office Expense	50	50	50	25	25	25	50	25	50	50	50	50	500
Print/Adv.	0	0	0	100	0	100	200	0	0	0	100	0	500
Total	4425	4675	4650	4475	4400	4150	4800	5175	4625	4700	5400	4925	56400
Monthly Total	-395	-645	-620	+65	+135	+390	-265	-645	+405	+1335	+135	+105	0
Cumulative Total	-395	-1040	-1660	-1595	-1460	-1070	-1335	-1980	-1575	-240	-105	0	

Figure 4.2 / Cash Flow Budget with Cumulative Totals. This budget is the same as in Figure 4.1 with the addition of a line showing the cumulative surplus/deficit.

Missions Fund Cash Flow Budget—FY '9___
Church Name
Address

	JAN	FEB	MAR	APR	MAY	JUN	JUL	AUG	SEP	OCT	NOV	DEC	TOTAL
INCOME:													
Mission Off.	1000	750	1000	1000	1000	1000	650	700	700	1000	1100	1100	11000
Trans from GF	400	400	400	450	450	450	450	450	500	600	550	500	5600
Total Income	1400	1150	1400	1450	1450	1450	1100	1150	1200	1600	1650	1600	16600
DISBURSEMENTS:													
Foreign Missions													
T. Jones	100	100	100	100	100	100	100	100	100	100	100	100	1200
T. Albert	100	100	100	100	100	100	100	100	100	100	100	100	1200
W. Smith	100	100	100	100	100	100	100	100	100	100	100	100	1200
S. Colbert	100	100	100	100	100	100	100	100	100	100	100	100	1200
D. Hankins	100	100	100	100	100	100	100	100	100	100	100	100	1200
T. Milford	50	50	50	50	50	50	50	50	50	50	50	50	600
Mission Off.	25	25	25	25	25	25	25	25	25	25	25	25	300
Total Foreign	575	575	575	575	575	575	575	575	575	575	575	575	6900
Home Missions:													
Boston	75	75	75	75	75	75	75	75	75	75	75	75	900
Worcester	75	75	75	75	75	75	75	75	75	75	75	75	900
Springfield	75	75	75	75	75	75	75	75	75	75	75	75	900
New Church Fund	25	25	25	25	25	25	25	25	25	25	25	25	300
Special Project	50	50	50	50	50	50	50	50	50	50	50	50	600
Total Home	300	300	300	300	300	300	300	300	300	300	300	300	3600
Other:													
Bible College	250	250	250	250	1250	250	250	250	250	250	250	250	4000
Miss. Speak/Hosp.	300	0	0	300	0	300	300	0	0	0	0	0	1200
Miss. Conference	0	0	0	0	0	0	0	0	0	900	0	0	900
Total Other	550	250	250	550	1250	550	550	250	250	1150	250	250	6100
Monthly Totals:	-25	+25	+275	+25	-675	+25	-325	+25	+75	-425	+525	+475	0

Figure 4.3 / Missions Cash Flow Budget. This shows how a cash flow budget can be useful for a subsidiary budget.

shows there will not be enough money at that time to pay for it, you can decide ahead of time whether the deficit should be met by having a special fund-raising event, by changing the timing of an already planned fund-raising event, by changing the timing of the expenditure, or by incurring some short-term or long-term indebtedness. Regardless of which course of action you decide on, you can compute the amount that will be needed and adjust the budget to reflect the decision.

If you decide on incurring debt instead of raising income, you can determine the length of time you will need to repay it. Sometimes you can arrange to pay for "big ticket" items in sixty or ninety days without having to pay interest. Your cash flow budget will help determine if you can pay on that schedule. If you cannot, you will know it ahead of time and will not make a promise which you cannot keep.

Summary

A cash flow budget breaks the annual budget into monthly increments to help you ensure sufficient cash will be available throughout the year to meet expected expenses when they arise. It helps you plan the timing of expenses or special income producing programs so that you can meet your cash flow requirements.

If you have a small church and you are a one-man budget committee, you still need a cash flow budget. You will have personally developed the annual budget and made estimates of the timing for each item of income and expense, so you can produce and use a cash flow budget the same way a large church would—and reap the same benefits.

It is not enough to have the necessary assets to cover your expected liabilities. You must have enough cash assets to meet the cash disbursement requirements at specific times if you are going to pay your bills on time and maintain a good testimony in your community.

If you have a small church and you are a one-man budget committee, you still need a cash flow budget.

Chapter 5

Seest thou a man diligent in his business? he shall stand before kings; he shall not stand before mean men.

—Proverbs 22:29

Making the Budget Work

The planning stage of budgeting is completed when the church accepts the budget for the new year. Developing a budget that can be used to benefit and guide the church has been hard work. However, budgets are developed to be used—they do not operate themselves. Unless church leaders actively look at the budget regularly and use it as a "road map" to guide financial operations as it is intended, the entire budget development process has been a wasted effort. The effectiveness of your budget operation depends entirely on two things: (1) your planning, and (2) your "will-power," or character.

The effectiveness of your budget operation depends entirely on two things: (1) your planning, and (2) your "will-power," or character.

Taking Action

As in other areas of real life, you must begin by acting on the plan. After that you must evaluate the results as they occur and replan when it becomes necessary.

If you were diligent and thorough in developing the budget, you will have eliminated the majority of the difficulties that can arise to cause problems in your financial operations. However, remember that budgeting is a process, not an action. As in other areas of real life, you must begin by acting on the plan. After that you must evaluate the results as they occur and replan when it becomes necessary.

Since good budgets are meant to be guides and not absolute controls on the people who operate them, the financial manager who is responsible for seeing that the church stays on its budget's course must be able to tell the difference between a serious deviation that requires replanning action and a minor deviation that will probably take care of itself. Remember, you used your "best guess" (your estimate) when stating income and expenses during the budget planning process, so you cannot expect your actual income and expense amounts to be exactly as shown in your budget. The budget is only your estimate of what is going to happen; it does not guarantee that events will happen as you planned.

The financial manager . . . must be able to tell the difference between a serious deviation that requires replanning action and a minor deviation that will probably take care of itself.

The financial manager must have a complete and broad view of the church's goals for the year and the basic assumptions that underlie each of the budget estimates if he is going to be able to tell when the budget deviations are serious or minor. Because the pastor has the best grasp of the broad picture, he is the one who usually will decide if replanning action is necessary. Even if the church is large enough to have a business manager or has a lay-person who actually supervises church financial operations, the pastor should be aware of the financial progress of the church so he can detect serious budget deviations if they occur and can direct replanning (rebudgeting) action just as he directed the original budgeting process.

The pastor . . . is the one who usually will decide if replanning action is necessary.

The actual dollar amount of what is a serious deviation will be different for every church. Some churches would be in serious difficulty if their income were $500 lower for the month than expected or if an unexpected $500 expense arose. Other churches have developed reserve funds for such emergencies and would handle the situation as a minor deviation that does not require action. The pastor or financial manager must be able to evaluate the situation, not only the deviation amount but also the cause and the likelihood of it happening again, and take the appropriate action.

Money management is both an art and a science. You can set down the factual numbers, but evaluating what they mean requires a degree of creativity and understanding that goes beyond mere facts, or science. Evaluating financial facts and using them to determine appropriate action is an art that is developed with practice over a period of time.

Of course, without willpower, or the character and determination to live within the budget, no amount of skill in planning will make a budget useful. Deviations from the budget that require replanning should be caused by unforeseen circumstances, not by lack of determination on the part of the financial manager to live within the budget.

An office manager should not be allowed to buy a "faster" computer if the purchase is not in the budget. If a fire in the church office destroyed the old computer, then you would probably have to replan the budget and buy a new one. Buying a new computer in the first case would show lack of character or determination; the second case illustrates an unforeseen event that could not have been planned for but must be accommodated.

Using the Budget

The cash flow budget is the tool a financial manager uses most often during the course of the year to help make the routine financial decisions that constantly arise. If he can stay close to each of those monthly estimates, he knows he will be close to the annual totals.

At the beginning of each month, the financial manager should review how the actual operation for the

> The actual dollar amount of what is a "serious" deviation will be different for every church.

> Without willpower, or the character and determination to live within the budget, no amount of skill in planning will make a budget useful.

> The cash flow budget is the tool the financial manager uses most often . . . to help make . . . routine financial decisions.

previous month compares to the cash flow budget for that month. The monthly financial statement the bookkeeper prepares for the church shows the actual income and disbursements for the month,[1] and is useful for keeping the church informed and for planning upcoming budgets. In addition, it is also good to prepare a monthly budget comparison report that shows what the actual income and disbursements were versus the budgeted amounts for each item of income and expense for the same month and for the year to date (fig. 5.1). This report helps the pastor or financial manager determine how well they are doing in relation to the plan for the month and for the year so far.

You should also use the cash flow budget to look at the upcoming month. This preview will remind you of non-routine or unusual income or expenses you have planned for the upcoming month so you are prepared for them when they happen. There may be a larger than usual bank balance at the beginning of the month, but this may be the month when you are planning to buy a new piece of expensive equipment—which would explain why there is a larger than usual bank balance at the beginning of the month. All of this is reflected in your cash flow budget. Whatever the circumstances, previewing the cash flow budget will remind you of the things you have planned for the new month so you can decide whether you are going to carry through with the original plan or need to adjust it to suit the current circumstances.

Developing the Budget Comparison Report

A budget comparison report is easily prepared:
- Copy the information from the cash flow budget for the appropriate month into the Budget column

1. Jack A. Henry, *Basic Accounting for Churches* (Nashville, Tenn.: Broadman & Holman Publishers, 1994) chap. 9, "Financial Reports and Audits."

BUDGET COMPARISON REPORT
Church Name
Address
General Fund March 199_

	March Budget	March Actual	March Variance	Year to Date Budget	Year to Date Actual	Year to Date Variance
INCOME:						
Regular Offering	$4,000.00	$4,150.00	$-150.00	$12,000.00	$12,465.00	$-465.00
Interest	30.00	29.00	1.00	90.00	92.00	-2.00
TOTAL	$4,030.00	$4,179.00	$-149.00	$12,090.00	$12,557.00	$-467.00
DISBURSEMENTS:						
Staff Salaries	$1,250.00	$1,250.00	$0.00	$3,250.00	$3,250.00	$0.00
Staff Car Exp.	250.00	225.00	25.00	700.00	650.00	50.00
Staff Housing	750.00	750.00	0.00	2,250.00	2,250.00	0.00
Mortgage Payment	900.00	900.00	0.00	2,700.00	2,700.00	0.00
Missions Transfer	400.00	415.00	-15.00	1,200.00	1,246.50	-46.50
Utilities	800.00	750.00	50.00	2,600.00	2,500.00	100.00
Sunday School	150.00	140.00	10.00	250.00	210.00	40.00
Building Insurance	0.00	0.00	0.00	375.00	375.00	0.00
Building Maintenance	50.00	52.00	-2.00	200.00	195.00	5.00
Janitor Supplies	50.00	35.00	15.00	75.00	67.00	8.00
Office Expense	50.00	50.00	0.00	150.00	146.00	4.00
Print/Advertising	0.00	0.00	0.00	0.00	0.00	0.00
TOTAL	$4,650.00	$4,567.00	$83.00	$13,750.00	$13,589.50	$160.50
Total	$-620.00	$-388.00	$-232.00	$-1,660.00	$-1,032.50	$-627.50

Figure 5.1 / Actual vs. Budget Comparison Report. This report compares how the actual income and disbursements compare to the budgeted amounts. It shows the comparison for the month and also for the year to date.

- Copy the information from the monthly financial statement into the Actual column
- Subtract the Actual column from the Budget column for each budget item
- Enter the results in the Variance column.

The Year to Date columns contain the cumulative totals for each budget item. They are prepared by adding this month's Budget or Actual amount to the respective Year to Date amount shown on the budget comparison report for the previous month. For example, to prepare the report for March shown in figure 5.1, you would simply add the amount in the March Budget column to the amount in the corresponding Year to Date column on February's budget comparison report.

Evaluating the Information

After having done the arithmetic and completing the budget comparison report, you can tell at a glance if any item of income or expense was either over or under budget. If the number in the Variance column is negative then the actual income or expense for that item was more than the amount budgeted for the month. If the number in the Variance column has no sign, it is a positive number and that item was under budget. Of course, it would be nice if all income items were negative in the Variance column and all expense items positive. That would mean that you were over budget in all income categories and under budget in all expense categories—you would be doing better in every category than expected.

If you want variance computed in percentages rather than dollars, computer accounting software can do it. It will show either the monthly or year-to-date variance from budget expectations for each item expressed in percent of the item's budget. This is somewhat useful if you are fluent with numbers and can mentally calculate what the percentage numbers are telling you, but it is not very helpful if you are not fluent with numbers.

If you are fluent with numbers and decide to have the variances expressed in percent, you may be able to use the Management by Exception (MBE) principle and only investigate budget items that exceed some percent of variance that you have set. Remember, however, a 5 percent variance from a $1,000 budget item is only $50, but a 5 percent variance from a $100,000 budget item (such as a year-to-date total for general fund offerings) is $5,000. As a general rule, it is usually easier to gain the budget management information you want from your budget comparison report if you express the variances in dollar numbers instead of in percents.

Remember, you were conservative when estimating income, so you should expect sometimes to be over budget in income. Also, you were liberal when you estimated expenses, so you should expect sometimes to be under budget in some expenses. You, as manager, must be the judge of whether, or when, you have been too conservative or too liberal when making estimates. Usually, you will be close enough to the budget so you do not need to make adjustments. However, you will be able to use the knowledge you gain to help make better estimates in the future.

Surplus Income

When reviewing the information from the budget comparison report and looking at the cash flow budget for the next month, you might notice that the growth in income you planned for the year is ahead of schedule while you are about right on target with expenses. You would have several options for dealing with this circumstance.

1. You could be conservative and assign all unplanned excess income to a reserve fund to be considered for use at some later date.

   a. You might decide to do this for three or four months to make sure the trend is real. If it continues, then you could revise the annual budget by:

      (1) increasing an item of expense, or

      (2) by adding a new item of expense that you had not included in the budget because it did not have high enough priority.

> It is usually easier to gain the budget management information you want from your budget comparison report if you express the variances in dollar numbers instead of in percents.

> You, as manager, must be the judge of whether, or when, you have been too conservative or too liberal when making estimates.

b. You might decide to let this accumulate in the reserve fund for the entire year and deal with it during the next budget cycle.

2. You could still be conservative by deciding to use some of the excess income to buy items that are already budgeted but are planned to be purchased later in the year. *Note:* This will change your cash flow budget, but not your annual budget.

Excess Expense

Your Cash Flow Budget will help you decide whether you can merely adjust the timing of spending or if you will have to change your annual budget.

Your budget comparison report might also show the opposite—expenses might be more than planned and income about what you expected. In that case, you have to adjust spending to fit income. Again, your cash flow budget will help you decide whether you can merely adjust the timing of spending, or if you will have to change your annual budget.

1. If you decide to adjust the timing of spending, then make the corrections to your cash flow budget that are necessary and go on with the new plan. Remember, changing the timing of your spending only changes the cash flow budget, not the annual budget.

2. If you decide that you must also reduce the amount of planned spending in the annual budget, then use both your annual budget and your cash flow budget to determine what items of spending remain that can be considered for reduction or elimination. Refer back to the written goals and priorities that you used originally to develop your budget and select items to eliminate from the bottom of your priority list until enough are eliminated to balance the budget.

3. You might also decide that rather than eliminate any item from the budget, you will put forth a special effort to increase income. You might consider doing this by having a special fund drive or by initiating a long-term growth plan for income.

The decision about which type of action is needed is made easier by using the cash flow budget to determine whether there will be a critical cash flow problem in the immediate future, or if the deficit is growing slowly and can be cured by a long-term plan. In any event, your annual budget and cash flow budget are "road maps" to help you stay on course toward achieving your goals. Your budget comparison report will help you determine when, or if, you get off course and where the problem is. By using all three of these documents, you can determine how to get back on course.

Remember, the goals you are working to achieve are spiritual goals—ministries—and the budget is merely the representation of those goals in dollars and cents. If you operate within your budget, you are making provision to achieve your ministry goals. If you do not, you are not.

Budgets, comparisons, and reports help you determine your condition, but you must evaluate the information they provide and decide what to do about it. If your planning is good, you may not have to do anything all year but follow the plan—and your character will determine whether you will.

> If you operate within your budget, you are making provision to achieve your ministry goals. If you do not, you are not.

Handling Emergencies

Financial emergencies should arise only from completely unforeseeable situations. Good budgeting takes care of all situations that can be expected under normal conditions.

Financial emergencies are usually thought of as crises caused by expenses that are beyond the financial capability of the church. However, a particularly good opportunity for ministry may present itself at an unexpected time and the church is without the financial means to pursue it. In either case, these are financial emergencies and you have several options.

1. You can raise a special offering to satisfy the particular need. This may be an opportunity to grow the faith of some members of your congregation as they are challenged to give sacrificially. You do

not want to do this too often or for inconsequential reasons—your people will resent it. If you seem to have to do this frequently, it is probably because you do not plan well.

2. You can reduce the budget in another area to have the money for the unexpected need.

3. The "emergency" may be for something that you can do without. Your original budget priorities will help you make up your mind.

In general, procedures for handling emergencies are the same as those you use when evaluating monthly budget progress. Your budget, which has already been developed, represents your decisions about priorities for the church's ministries during the budget year. Your annual budget is your map for the year, and your cash flow budget is your map for the short-term—both of them help you achieve overall objectives for the highest priority ministries.

> There are times when it is prudent to gain approval before making planned budget adjustments.

Approving Revisions

Budget operation and changes have been discussed from the financial manager's viewpoint. Even though the church may have approved the budget as a guide rather than as an absolute limit for each budget item, there are times when it is prudent to gain approval before making planned budget adjustments. The pastor or financial manager should be given great leeway to operate within the spirit and intent of the budget—the written objectives and priorities as well as the numerical figures. However, when budget variances become serious he should bring them to the church's attention. After all, the financial needs of the church are the concern of the entire congregation, not just the pastor or financial manager.

> Good leadership and the desire to maintain a good testimony in financial operations dictates that the church should review and approve major budget deviations.

Sometimes the church bylaws will state specific limits for budget variances beyond which specified approval action is required. Even when this is not the case, good leadership and the desire to maintain a good testimony in financial operations dictates that the church should review and approve major budget deviations. The appropriate organizational level for review may be the finance committee, the church board, or even the church itself. The determining factors are the seriousness of the deviation from the approved budget and the cause of the deviation.

If the utility bills are consistently higher than planned, but their overrun is not causing cuts to any other budget item, then probably no action is necessary. You might mention the budget overrun when you give the next monthly financial report to the church, but no real approval action is needed. If the computer you budgeted for went up in price so much that you will have to postpone purchasing another approved budget item, you may want to discuss it with the finance committee and secure approval before going ahead with the purchase. If the air conditioner breaks down unexpectedly in mid-August and is not reparable, and the purchase of a new air conditioner will mean cutting a substantial amount from another ministry area, then the readjustment of the annual budget should probably be referred to the whole church. Each of these situations requires a management decision by the chief financial manager, usually the pastor.

> The pastor must recognize that the entire congregation is responsible for the church's financial affairs and must be kept informed if they are to pray and act as they should.

Even though church policy should allow the pastor or financial manager great leeway in operating the budget, the pastor must recognize that the entire congregation is responsible for the church's financial affairs and must be kept informed if they are to pray and act as they should. He must exercise his authority as a manager to make decisions and not burden the church with petty details, but he must keep the church informed.

Summary

Because the budget represents the expected giving of the people and the dollar costs of your church's highest ministry priorities for the year, you should be motivated to operate within the budget. Making the budget work for you depends on your planning, or budgeting ability, and on your determination to stick to your plan. There is nothing magic about the budget that will cause it to operate itself—the financial manager must manage it.

The annual budget should be broken down into monthly components to form a cash flow budget. This ensures that the timing of your planned expenditures coincides with the timing of your income, so you will know that you will have enough cash on hand to pay your bills on time. Because the cash flow budget reflects your plan for each month's operation, it is the tool most used to control current spending.

To keep a constant check on how you are doing, you should compare the monthly financial statement that shows actual financial operations for the month with the appropriate month's cash flow budget. Minor variations between the two should be expected because your budget was based on estimates, but major variations indicate problems that demand management action. Distinguishing between a major and a minor variation requires a management decision that must be made honestly so that appropriate action can be taken. Remember, making the budget work requires not only good planning, but also the willpower and character to stay within the plan.

When unforeseeable circumstances arise, then changes to the budget must be made. Determining what changes are necessary and how to make them is made easier by the work done during the budget development process. If budgeted items must be reduced or eliminated from the budget, the list of priorities developed during the budgeting process will help you decide what specific action is necessary. If an unexpected surplus becomes available, the same priority list will help you determine how to handle it. Remember, the budget is a road map to help guide you through the year to where you want to be at the end. Let it work for you.

Chapter 6

*There is treasure to be desired and oil in the dwelling of
the wise; but a foolish man spendeth it up.*

—*Proverbs 21:20*

Spending

Good spending habits are vital to good money management. Just because an item is in the budget does not mean that you absolutely must buy it or pay the exact price that is budgeted. Having an item in the budget represents your best estimate of what is needed—actual circumstances at the time will dictate whether your estimate was correct.

Too often, inexperienced financial managers treat the budget as the "ruler" and not as the "guide," especially when it comes to buying something they want. Once again, remember that budgets guide spending, but people control it. When it is time to spend money on a budgeted item, it is time to determine if the item is actually necessary.

A friend with over thirty years on the mission field once gave me his personal guideline for controlling spending. It might seem a bit too conservative, but it at

Good spending habits are vital to good money management.

When it is time to spend money on a budgeted item, it is time to determine if the item is actually necessary.

least demonstrates the key elements you should consider when deciding if you will purchase any item, even if it is in the budget. His rule was: Use it up, wear it out, make it do, or do without.

Spending Guidelines

Every expenditure requires a decision to spend and the budget is only a guide for helping make that decision. For example, when you developed your budget, your best estimate of the church's needs included replacing that old vacuum cleaner that was on its last legs and could not possibly last past March, so money for a new one is in the March budget. However, the last time the janitor tinkered with it he resuscitated it, and it is now running like a charm. There is no reason to automatically buy a new vacuum cleaner just because it is in the approved budget. You should have a procedure to evaluate the situation at the time; determine if it is used up, worn out, etc.; and act (spend) accordingly.

Just as you have policies and procedures for conducting worship services, receiving offerings, and developing the budget, you should also have standard policies and procedures for spending money. Your policies are general guidelines, and your procedures spell out the step-by-step actions that are required to make a purchase. Both should be written so everyone knows what to do when he or she wants to buy something, but do not bog them down with too many details. Written policies and procedures help you make decisions to actually spend money, and also help you train new people.

Guideline # 1: Centralized Control

The Purchasing Agent. Designate one person as the purchasing agent to approve all purchases, and do not allow anybody to spend cash or charge anything to the church's accounts without his or her specific authorization. The purchasing agent should be the same person who controls the budget—usually the pastor. If the church is large enough to have a business manager,

Every expenditure requires a decision to spend, and the budget is only a guide for helping make that decision.

Designate one person as the purchasing agent to approve all purchases, and do not allow anybody to spend cash or charge anything to the church's accounts without his or her specific authorization.

SPENDING GUIDELINES

1. Centralized Control
2. Included in Budget
3. Let Users Be Choosers
4. Buy Locally If Possible
5. Buy General Merchandise
6. Buy in Quantity and Save
7. Buy Seasonal and Sales Goods
8. Test New Products in Small Quantities
9. Provide for Proper Receiving

Figure 6.1 / Spending Guidelines. These guidelines should be considered when developing policies and procedures to control spending.

then he should be the purchasing agent. This individual knows what is in the budget and the cash flow plan. He also knows how well the actual financial status coincides with the budget. Because of his general knowledge of the overall financial picture, he is best able to determine the appropriateness of any purchase.

Vendors. Most churches have charge accounts with vendors with whom they frequently do business. Charging something to a charge account is the same as spending cash for the item—it must eventually be paid for from the church's cash resources. Therefore, you must control the use of charge accounts the same way you control writing checks.

Charging something to a charge account is the same as spending cash for the item.

I know of a church that allowed all of its Sunday School teachers and officers—approximately forty people—to charge things for their classes and departments at local stores. The church had a good reputation and had been a landmark in the community for many years, so teachers could make purchases in almost any store in town merely by saying, "Charge it." This was very convenient for the teachers, but the church treasurer never knew what to expect in the way of monthly bills.

Every vendor should know that you will not pay for any purchase charged to your account unless it has been authorized by the purchasing agent—make sure the vendor knows who your purchasing agent is. This does not mean that the only person who can "go to the store" is the purchasing agent; it only means that the purchasing agent is the only one who can say what can be charged to the church when someone "goes to the store." Church staff personnel and Sunday School teachers can get approval for purchases, either verbal approval or with a formal purchase order, and then go make the purchases. If the approval is verbal, however, the purchasing agent must make sure he contacts the vendor and OK's the purchase so the vendor will charge the merchandise as authorized.

Having one central purchasing agent also helps in other ways. His frequent contact with the church's vendors makes him aware of the level of service each provides. Also, he often develops special relationships that result in the church getting the best of service, advance notice on special sales, and timely cost and service adjustments when appropriate.

Authority to Purchase. The purchasing agent deals mostly with purchases made for the church's operational needs—office supplies, Sunday School materials, bus repairs, etc. In order to give him the leeway needed for efficient operation, he should be granted authority to spend as necessary but within the limits of the annual budget. With specified limits, he should also be given additional authority to deviate from the budget without referral to any committee or the church if the deviation is within the budget's stated objectives and priorities. This additional authority allows him to continue paying utility bills and carry on routine business even when actual costs or prices vary from the budgeted amounts. If these variances become significant, he should inform the church.

Deciding if a price change can be accommodated within the budget guidelines is an executive decision which the purchasing agent should make. If a purchasing agent exceeds his authority when making those kinds of decisions, and does so repeatedly, then corrective personnel action should be taken. However, he should not be prevented from doing his job by not giving him the authority he needs to do it. The general principle is to provide for efficient financial management within budget guidelines without having to continually resort to committee action.

Capital purchases such as land, buildings, vehicles, etc., usually require specific approval by either the church board or the church itself. This approval may be given when the church approves the budget if the specific item is in the budget; however, legal requirements may call for specific signatures or other actions. More than normal church participation in the mechanics of making large capital purchases is not unusual. Even if not required, it is good procedure to secure specific approval for major expenditures and capital investments, and the church's purchasing agent should be responsible for initiating the request and secure the appropriate approval.

Guideline #2: Included in Budget

Checking the budget should be the first action in deciding all spending questions. If the desired item is not in the budget, do not buy it unless it is so vital that it is worth initiating action to revise the budget.

If the purchasing agent always asks the person making the spending request, "Is it in the budget?" he or she will begin to check the budget before asking.

In every case when the answer is no, the purchasing agent's automatic response should be, "Then put it in your budget request for next year, and we will discuss adding it to next year's budget. We can't buy it this year because you didn't ask for it, and therefore we didn't consider it."

By doing this, the purchasing agent will reinforce the importance of the budget process, encourage managers to do their best when developing their budgets, and maintain the integrity of the current budget.

Of course, there can always be expenditures that are worthy of causing budget replanning action—that is why the budget is a guide and not the master. Determining when to replan is a judgment call that the pastor or financial manager must make. Staying within the

The general principle is to provide for efficient financial management within budget guidelines without having to continually resort to committee action.

It is good procedure to secure specific approval for major expenditures and capital investments.

Checking the budget should be the first action in deciding all spending questions.

Determining when to replan is a judgment call.

budget will get easier and requests to purchase items not in the budget will diminish as all of the staff, teachers, superintendents and other workers become experienced at working within the budget.

Guideline #3: Let Users Be Choosers

The people who are doing the work should have an opportunity to help select the material they are going to work with. In the budget development process you gave the people submitting budget requests opportunity to specify vendors, brands, etc., on their budget request forms. If at all possible, honor those requests. If you cannot purchase the specific item they requested for any reason, give them an opportunity to select a substitute. Just as people carry out their own ideas and suggestions best, they will generally be happier and more productive if you honor their preference regarding supplies and equipment.

There may be legitimate reasons why you can't honor their preferences—cost, availability, etc.—but honor them if you can.

Guideline #4: Buy Locally If Possible

The more exposure you, your church, and your church members have in the personal, business, and community life of your town, the wider will be your field of ministry.

There are a number of reasons why you should buy locally if possible. The first and most obvious is that your church is part of a community, and you should participate in it as much as possible. The more exposure you, your church, and your church members have in the personal, business, and community life of your town, the wider your field of ministry will be.

If your church is in a small town, you may not have the variety of vendors that are available in larger cities. Small town stores tend to charge higher prices than large super-stores and national mail order houses, but their prices will often include transportation costs, thereby reducing the total cost of an item. A local store may also provide better service for the equipment you buy from them than you would receive from some distant provider.

Many times the convenience, availability, and quality of service is well worth some added initial cost. Price is not the only consideration when buying supplies and equipment, and buying locally may provide valuable benefits that are not included in the ticket price.

Guideline #5: Buy General Merchandise

Some items are used almost exclusively by churches and are generally available only from vendors of church supplies and equipment. Church pews, altar furniture, and offering plates are examples. On the other hand, most supplies and items of equipment that are used by churches are also used by the general public. As a rule, items of general public use are cheaper in price than the same item identified as being specifically for a church.

"Choir chairs" are often more expensive than similar chairs in a secular store. Church computer software for bookkeeping and attendance records is often more expensive than software designed to do the same thing in a secular setting. As a general rule, base your purchases on what the supplies and equipment will do, not on what they are called.

Guideline #6: Buy in Quantity and Save

You are often able to get a lower price if you buy in large quantities. In addition to a price break, you can often save on shipping costs. Sometimes a vendor will pay shipping costs if you buy a certain quantity, and shipping costs today often run 5 percent or more of the invoice amount.

Types of things you might consider buying in quantity are janitorial supplies, paper for the copier, offering envelopes, etc. Be careful, though, that you do not buy too large a quantity of an item just to get a price break. I was in a church, once, with a ten-year supply of adding machine tape, and nobody knew what to do with it.

Remember that you have to store your supplies and equipment where they are not in your way, will not get used for unintended purposes, and where they are protected from damage. The amount of proper storage space you have may sometimes limit your ability to take advantage of volume discounts.

Guideline #7: Buy Seasonal and Sales Goods

Some types of supplies and equipment are traditionally lower in price at certain times of the year. Automobiles are usually cheaper at the model change time, snow blowers are cheaper in the spring, and lawn mowers in the fall. If possible, plan your cash flow budget to take advantage of the lower prices.

When taking advantage of sales prices you must still stay within your annual budget guidelines.

You can often save considerable amounts of money by taking advantage of sales on items of all kinds. Remember, though, when taking advantage of sales prices you must still stay within your annual budget guidelines, and you do not want to overstock to the point of causing yourself a storage problem.

Guideline #8: Test New Products in Small Quantities

Churches are notorious for having loose purchasing procedures, so they are targets for all kinds of salesmen and sales promotions. These promotions are often for new products that require large quantity purchases. Regardless of the promised benefits, do not buy large amounts of anything you have not tried and proven for yourself. New or old products may not work as advertised in your particular application—or they may be better than advertised. In any event, make sure all products you buy in large quantities are going to do the job you expect of them.

Do not accept merchandise you have not ordered, and do not pay for merchandise you ordered but did not receive.

Guideline #9: Provide for Proper Receiving

Two important issues are involved with having proper receiving procedures. You do not want to accept merchandise you have not ordered, and you do not want to pay for merchandise you ordered but did not receive.

The Shipping Document. When you receive merchandise shipped to you, there is usually a shipping document included or attached to the container. This shipping document lists the contents of the package and gives you a convenient record to use to verify that the package actually contained exactly what is listed. When opening a box of supplies or equipment you have ordered, use the following checklist:

1. Take everything out of the box and make sure there are no small items left in the packing material.

2. Using the shipping document, verify that the proper quantity, size, color, etc., of each item shown on the shipping document was actually in the box.

3. Check off each item on the shipping document as you verify it so when you are finished, you have a record of exactly what you received.

4. If there were any discrepancies between the contents and the document, describe the discrepancies on the shipping document.

5. Put the date you checked the shipment and your signature or initials on the document when you finish so it is apparent who verified the shipment.

After marking your verification of the contents on the shipping document, check your purchase order against the verified shipping document to insure that you received everything you ordered, or there is a note about missing items being back ordered. (If you do not use a purchase order system, you still should have a list of what you ordered and when.) Attach the shipping document to the purchase order and give it to the bookkeeper. When he gets the invoice, or bill, from the vendor, he will know that the merchandise was received. The purchasing agent should not authorize the bookkeeper to pay any invoice until receipt of the merchandise is verified.

The purchasing agent should not authorize the bookkeeper to pay any invoice until receipt of the merchandise is verified.

In addition to counting and verifying the items that are received, good receiving procedures include putting the items received into their proper storage locations. Supplies left sitting around usually disappear. If they do not reach the people for whom they were purchased, you may as well not have bought them.

Scam Warning. A sales scam that is continually in operation around the country involves shipping you merchandise you did not order and then billing you for it. When you receive a shipment of any kind, you ought to immediately look for the purchase order to verify that the items were actually ordered. If you did not order it, do not accept it, and do not pay for it.

A variation on this scheme is to send only a bill for merchandise and not the merchandise itself. Many churches have such poor control of their receiving function that they just assume they received the material and go ahead and pay the bill. The simple procedure of verifying the contents of shipments, matching verified shipping documents with purchase orders, and requiring them to be attached before any bill is paid will preclude your being taken in by either of these frauds.

Good receiving procedures include putting the items received into their proper storage locations. Supplies left sitting around usually disappear.

Purchase Orders

When a church gets so large that more than one person is making a substantial number of purchases, it may be time to implement a purchase order system. However, with tight controls on the spending function exercised by a single purchasing agent, some large churches and Christian organizations operate very efficiently and effectively without using purchase orders. If the purchase order system is not used, you must maintain a file of whatever other form is used in its place to show how much money has been obligated by making charge purchases and what the charges were for.[1]

The purchase order system will help you in several ways.

1. It will help you control the actual authorization of purchases.

2. It will serve as a written notice to the vendor that the church has authorized the particular purchase.

1. Jack A. Henry, *Basic Accounting for Churches* (Nashville, Tenn.: Broadman & Holman, 1994), 115.

3. It will assist you in verifying the receipt of items you have ordered.

4. It will aid you in keeping track of the amount of money you have obligated but have not yet been billed for.[2]

The standard purchase order form contains information about a specific purchase so that the vendor and the church purchasing agent know exactly what is being authorized for purchase. The forms are standard business forms that can be bought in almost any office supply store or office supply section of a department store. Many office supply stores will customize them for you and put your church name and logo on the form for a small charge. You can even design your own form on your computer so that the purchase order can also be used as a "purchase request form." (See fig. 6.2.) The standard form can also be used as a request form by requiring the requestor to sign it signifying that he has checked the budget and verified the appropriateness of the purchase as discussed below. Regardless of the kind you use, each form should show the following.

1. Date
2. Church name, address and phone number
3. Purchase order number
4. Information about the purchase—
    a. The name and address of the vendor
    b. The quantity being authorized of each item being purchased
    c. A description of each item
    d. The unit price and total amount you are authorizing to be paid for each item
    e. The total amount of the purchase order
5. The name of the person requesting approval for the purchase order with space for his signature
6. The name of the person approving the purchase order with space for his signature
7. The date approved

---

2. Ibid.

PURCHASE ORDER

TO: *A.B.C Hardware*   SHIP TO: Church Name
         100 Main St.   Address
         Boston, MA.   Phone Number

DATE: *1/10/9–*   P.O. Number: *001*

Qty	Description	Unit Price	Total Price
1 ea.	Vacuum Cleaner Model c-14	49.95	49.95
1 doz.	Cleaning Cloth (per dozen)	5.40	5.40
		Grand Total	55.35

Requested by: *W.B. Tyler*
(Typed name & signature)

Authorized by: *J.B. Mark*
(Typed name & signature)   (Date)

Figure 6.2 / Purchase Order Form. The standard purchase order contains information about a specific purchase of one or more items.

Using Purchase Orders

Purchase order forms are used to originate requests to purchase items of supplies or equipment and are usually originated by a departmental superintendent or church staff member. Procedures vary but a common practice is to complete the form in triplicate, giving one copy to the vendor, one to the person making the purchase request, and one to the purchasing agent to file. Whatever procedures you develop to tailor the system to your church, keep them simple but adequate.[3]

After entering all of the required information on the purchase order form, and before submitting it for approval, the originator should check it against the approved annual budget to ensure that each item on the purchase order is there and also in the cash flow budget for the appropriate time period. If everything requested is in both the annual and the cash flow budgets, the requestor signs the form and submits it to the church's purchasing agent. The requestor's signature certifies that he has reviewed the budget and the purchase is appropriate.

When the purchasing agent receives a completed purchase request (it is a request until the purchasing agent signs it to authorize the purchase; then it becomes a purchase order), he, too, should verify its inclusion in the budget. He should also determine the actual need for the item and the availability of the cash to pay for it when payment will likely become due. If all is in order,

1. He signs the purchase order,

2. Logs it in the purchase order log,

3. Puts one copy in the purchase order file,

4. Returns two copies to the person making the request so that he can proceed with the purchase.

The basic purpose of the system is to control spending, so you will want to keep a record of each purchase order issued and whether it has been completed. Remember, your purchase order is an authorization to spend money, so maintaining tight control of the blank forms as well as the approved and completed purchase orders is very important.

A simple list, or log, of the purchase orders you have authorized, such as is illustrated in figure 6.3, is sufficient to maintain adequate control. This log will show

> The basic purpose of the [purchase order] system is to control spending.

---

3. Henry, *Basic Accounting*, 3.

you at a glance if a purchase in question has been authorized or received, and the dates each action occurred.

Once the purchase order is signed and logged, the purchaser takes it to the vendor to have the order filled. Sometimes the vendor is not local and the purchase order must be mailed, but the same principle applies. Even if the order is filled locally and the purchaser went to the store personally, selected the items, took them to the sales clerk and signed the charge ticket, the receiving procedures outlined above (pp. 76–77) should be followed.

If the requested items are not in the appropriate budgets, the requestor should note that fact on the face of the request and include additional information to show why the budget should be revised to accommodate the unbudgeted purchase request. Remember, everybody should be actively involved in making the approved budget work.

Neither teachers, superintendents, nor church staff should submit purchase order requests for unbudgeted items except in emergencies, and even then they should provide credible reasons why budget changes should be made. Repeat offenders should receive additional training regarding their financial responsibilities. If they continue to be unable or unwilling to exercise financial control over their areas of responsibility, other actions should be taken. Your leadership team must be made up of people who can be counted on to lead within the limits of the agreed-upon budget guidelines.

Summary

Budgets guide spending, but people control it. Budgets reflect your best estimate of what and when spending should occur, but actual circumstances are the controlling factors for actual spending. The utility bills may be higher or lower than you estimated, but your budget goal is to pay them on time. Therefore, the amount you pay for utilities depends on actual bills, not your budget.

Date Auth	P.O. #	Vendor/Remarks	Item Description	Total Price	Date Rec'd
		PURCHASE ORDER LOG			
		Church Name			
		Address			
1/15/9-	001	ABC Hardware (Back Order)	Vac. Cleaner; Clean Cloth	55.35	
1/15/9-	002	XYZ Office Supply	Paper, Pens, Binder	52.19	1/15/9-

Figure 6.3 / Purchase Order Log. This simple list of each purchase order and its status helps you maintain control of spending by controlling your purchase orders.

To use the budget as a guide, you must have centralized control of the spending function. Centralized control is easily achieved by designating one person to be the purchasing agent and requiring all purchases to be authorized by him. He must be given authority to spend within the guidelines of the budget's goals and priorities and not be held to the exact numbers in the budget if he is to maintain the flexibility desired in a good budget.

Deciding when replanning action is necessary is an executive decision that should be exercised by the pastor. If the pastor is not the designated purchasing agent, then the purchasing agent should be responsible for notifying him when situations arise that require replanning. The pastor should always be informed sufficiently about the state of the church's financial affairs to initiate action on his own if it is necessary, even if the purchasing agent has not requested it.

Policies and procedures for controlling spending should be written so that everyone who needs to make a purchase for the church knows how. Although written, there should be no more procedures than necessary, and the ones you have should be simple.

Many churches use purchase orders to help them control spending and provide other benefits as well. Other methods for authorizing and controlling spending can be used effectively to achieve the same results, but alternative methods should be designed to ensure that all of the benefits of the purchase order system are contained in them too.

Control of spending . . . is the responsibility of every worker and officer in the church.

Control of spending is not only the business of the pastor or purchasing agent—it is the responsibility of every worker and officer in the church. If an individual continually wants to buy things that he did not ask for during the budget development process, or that were asked for but not included in the budget, he should receive more training about his financial responsibilities and the church's procedures. If that does not change his actions, he should be replaced in his leadership position.

Financial management includes the functions of receiving, recording, budgeting, and spending.[4] Many church workers recognize the need for good policies and procedures regarding the first three but completely overlook the fourth: spending. However, loose spending policies and procedures can nullify all of the spiritual leadership and physical effort that went into the first three.

Good spending habits are vital to good money management.

---

4. Henry, *Basic Accounting*, 8.

Chapter 7

And they took him, and brought him unto Areopagus, saying, May we know what this new doctrine, whereof thou speakest, is?

For thou bringest certain strange things to our ears: we would know therefore what these things mean.

(For all the Athenians and strangers which were there spent their time in nothing else, but either to tell, or to hear some new thing.)

—Acts 17:19–21

Computers and Budgets

When Paul spoke on Mars Hill in Athens, his listeners were curious because they were hearing things they had never heard before. They were amazed at what Paul was telling them about the God of heaven. They recognized the reality of God's mighty works, but they did not comprehend the whole truth about His greatness and what He had done for them. They did not realize that they, too, could be partakers of the great salvation which they were seeking but only God provided.

Sometimes, the thought of using a computer is as strange an idea to a pastor as the gospel message was to the Athenians. Pastors and church workers are often curious about how computers are used in churches but do not think computers would be helpful for them. They recognize the benefits other churches enjoy from using computers but think that somehow they are excluded from enjoying those benefits.

The Computer's Role

A computer is a servant—nothing more. However, it is a very dependable servant. It will do only what you tell it to do, but it will follow your instructions faithfully without deviation, rapidly without error, and repeatedly without weariness.

Budgeting requires making and recording a lot of computations with meticulous accuracy. Often those computations must be written repeatedly in different locations. Computers are ideal for doing this mechanical work of computing and entering the numbers for budgeting and other accounting functions. They are also ideal for writing the policies, procedures, and reports associated with budgeting and accounting functions. In other words, they can do the work of the servant, but they cannot make the decisions. The thinking, praying, and decision making are still the work of human beings.

God uses people to accomplish His work, but He gives them tools to use to lighten the load. Computers are a modern-day tool to lighten the load.

The User's Role

One requirement for using computers that is often forgotten is that information must be put into the computer before anything can be gotten out. A computer is a "brain" that can only operate on the information you give it. When you decide to begin using computers to help in accounting, budgeting, letter writing, printing, etc., you have to plan to take the time to input the basic information into the computer that you expect it to work with. In addition, you should plan to take time to learn to use the software you will be working with. When you begin the process of converting to computers, you will find that investing the time to input your data and learning how to operate the software properly

A computer is a servant—nothing more. However, it is a very dependable servant.

Computers are a modern-day tool to lighten the load.

When you . . . begin using computers . . . you have . . . to take the time to input the basic information into the computer that you expect it to work with.

will pay off handsomely in the long run. You will get more from your computer and your time.

Things the computer needs to know before it can help you with your budget are: What will be included in the budget (what are the accounts you are going to budget for)? What accounts will you have in your bookkeeping system that are not included in your budget? And how do they relate to each other? You will have income accounts such as regular offering and missions offering; and expense accounts, such as salaries and office supplies for which you are going to make estimates to include in your budget. You will also have some accounts that you do not make estimates for in your budgeting process but which are necessary for your accounting records. Examples of these non-budget accounts are the checking account(s) and the fund balance accounts for each of the types of funds[1] you maintain. A list of all of these kinds of accounts is called a Chart of Accounts (app. A, fig. A.1) and must be input into the computer before it will generate the budget information you want.

The Market's Offerings

You do not have to buy the top-of-the-line computer with the biggest memory nor the most expensive church software for computers. Several good inexpensive accounting programs are on the market that are suitable for handling your church's accounting and budgeting. Base your decision about which computer hardware to buy on the decision about what software you want to run on it. Choosing the software is based on what you plan to use the computer for—do not limit yourself here; it will do a great variety of writing, record keeping, drawing, and printing chores for you as well as accounting and budgeting chores.

On the market are a number of inexpensive ($50–$200) computer bookkeeping programs used by

Base your decision about which computer hardware to buy on the decision about what software you want to run on it.

---

1. Jack A. Henry, *Basic Accounting for Churches* (Nashville, Tenn.: Broadman & Holman Publishers, 1994), 42.

churches that include features to help with budgeting. They can be found in most of your local computer software stores and often provide good technical support for new users. Remember, your software does not need to be specifically a "church bookkeeping program." All you need is a "bookkeeping program." Using the word *church* can add hundreds of dollars to the cost of the software. Almost all inexpensive bookkeeping programs can generate reports and graphs similar to those illustrated in appendix A.

The most popular inexpensive bookkeeping programs are easy to use (do not take a lot of man-hours of training to learn how), and include predefined reports you can use in your budgeting process and normal financial management functions. They will allow you to customize your reports to suit your specific needs and provide some graphics capability in the event you like to look at your financial information on piecharts or bar and line graphs.

Besides providing for quick and easy set-up of all of your accounts, good software will also have special procedures for making easy work of entering budget data. Of course, if you are going to use a cash flow budget (fig. 4.1) and monthly actual versus budget comparison reports (fig. 5.1), then you will have to enter monthly budget amounts. Once this budget data is entered, it can be used to compute other data for a variety of reports and graphic illustrations. It can also be easily changed when necessary and then viewed on the screen or printed out on paper. Doing this shows you the effect of proposed budget changes so you can understand their impact before making budget decisions to implement them. Remember, a computer is good at remembering, copying, and doing repetitive work—the kind of thing that saves you time and improves your accuracy.

Computer accounting programs offer another benefit: their ability to copy their output into other computer programs. This allows you to use the power of specialized database, spreadsheet, and word processing software to further enhance the data that you generate

> Remember, a computer is good at remembering, copying, and doing repetitive work—the kind of thing that saves you time and improves your accuracy.

from your accounting program. For example, the cash flow information in figure 4.1 was first generated in a bookkeeping program and then saved to disk in a computer format that my word processing program could use. I then used a word processing program to rearrange the data and customize the results in ways that are best accomplished by word processing programs.

Each of the graphic depictions in appendix A is based on graphics originally generated by an inexpensive computer bookkeeping program[2] from the financial data it had stored for Bible Baptist Church. Each chart and graph presents the data visually in different ways, but all of them are useful for management decision making.

Problems to Avoid

There are two easily avoidable problems you should be aware of when you have a computer in the church office. The first problem is allowing staff or church members to put copies of their pet programs on the church computer. Installing and using a program that you have not purchased on a computer is called "pirating" and violates copyright law—it is illegal! Software is purchased for one computer only. In addition, the practice often fills up the memory of your computer and may cause your primary programs to run slower. Also, of major importance, this practice exposes your computer system to the danger of computer "viruses."

Computer viruses come in many forms, but they all destroy the data you have worked hard to store in the computer's memory. Copying someone's contaminated disk and running the program is how computer viruses are spread. The best way to prevent them from getting into your computer's system is to quarantine the computer from the sources that carry them—programs that have not been checked to insure that they are virus free.

---

2. "MoneyCounts 8.0," Parsons Technology, One Parsons Drive, P.O. Box 100, Hiawatha, IA 52233-0100.

The second problem relates to the security of confidential information in your computer files. Do not leave the computer in an uncontrolled office location where anyone who knows how to turn on a computer can gain access to the confidential information you may have stored in your computer files. If you must leave the computer in an office that is sometimes unlocked, use computer programs that are inacessible without passwords. Many programs have this capability.

Summary

Computers are tools that can be used effectively by pastors and church workers to help with routine and repetitive chores, which will provide more time for ministry. Budgeting requires a lot of computations to be made and numbers to be entered and reentered into reports—activities that the computer is designed to do rapidly, accurately, and without complaint.

Allow time . . . to learn how to use [computer] software. . . .You will be well rewarded by the time you save and the quality of product you get from your computer system.

When bringing your church into the computer age, be sure to allow time at the beginning to enter all of the data the computer will need to do what you want it to do. Also, allow time for yourself and staff who will be operating the computer to learn how to use the software. If you will do those two things at the start, you will be well rewarded by the time you save and the quality of product you get from your computer system. If you skimp on either, you will pay the price in frustration and lack of productivity.

A computer is a very versatile tool. Do not be afraid to use it.

Appendix A

Computer Reports and Graphics

All of the reports and graphics shown in this annex are based on similar products that were originally generated by computer bookkeeping software.[1] Most standard bookkeeping programs have the potential of producing many more different reports and graphs, but these were chosen to illustrate the variety of helps available to the neophyte computer user of inexpensive computer software. There are several other companies that produce easy-to-use, inexpensive computer software. You will have to decide for yourself which software best fills your requirements.

Before deciding to buy any program, you should investigate the difficulty of operating it. Also, look at the

---

1. "Moneycounts 8.0," Parsons Technology, One Parsons Drive, P.O. Box 100, Hiawatha, IA 52233-0100.

products (reports, graphs, etc.) you can generate with the program to make sure they will satisfy your needs. Remember, cost is not the only issue. You will invest time and energy to learn the program you decide on, and additional time and energy to input the originally required information. Once you have begun, you do not want to have to change programs without a compelling reason for doing so.

The two main points are:

1. Computer software need not be expensive or difficult to use in order to produce beneficial reports and graphics for a church's financial managers.

2. A small investment of time and money can lead to a large return in financial management capability, reliability, and time savings in the long run.

Look at each of the reports and graphs in this appendix and visualize how it could help you develop and manage your church's budget. Remember, if you are already doing your accounting with a computer program, and the program includes budgeting capabilities, the data is already there for the program to generate budget projections, comparison reports, and graphs, without your having to do anything but "tell" it which report or graph you want.

Chart of Accounts
Church Name/Address

Account Number	Account Name	Account Type	Fund Name
50	Pilgrim Savings Bank	Checking	General Fund
100	Petty Cash	Cash	General Fund
200	Land	Other assets	General Fund
210	Equipment & Vehicles	Other assets	General Fund
220	Buildings	Other assets	General Fund
400	Regular Offering	Income	General Fund
401	Interest Income	Income	General Fund
410	Building Fund Offering	Income	Building Fund
420	Missions Offering	Income	Missions Fund
425	Transfer from Gen. Fund	Income	Missions Fund
500	General Fund	Fund balance	General Fund
510	Building Fund	Fund balance	Building Fund
520	Missions Fund	Fund balance	Missions Fund
600	Staff Salaries	Expense	General Fund
601	Staff Car Allowance	Expense	General Fund
602	Staff Housing Allowance	Expense	General Fund
603	Mortgage Payment	Expense	General Fund
610	GF Transfer to Missions	Expense	General Fund
615	Utilities	Expense	General Fund
620	Sunday School Expense	Expense	General Fund
625	Building Insurance	Expense	General Fund
630	Building Maintenance	Expense	General Fund
635	Janitor Supplies	Expense	General Fund
650	Office Expense	Expense	General Fund
660	Print/Advertising	Expense	General Fund
800	T. Jones	Expense	Missions Fund
810	T. Albert	Expense	Missions Fund
820	W. Smith	Expense	Missions Fund
830	S. Colbert	Expense	Missions Fund
840	D. Hankins	Expense	Missions Fund
850	T. Milford	Expense	Missions Fund
860	Missions Office	Expense	Missions Fund
900	Bible College	Expense	Missions Fund
905	Boston Mission	Expense	Missions Fund
910	Cambridge Mission	Expense	Missions Fund
915	Springfield Mission	Expense	Missions Fund
920	New Church Fund	Expense	Missions Fund
925	Special Project	Expense	Missions Fund
950	Mission Speaker	Expense	Missions Fund
955	Mission Conference Exp.	Expense	Missions Fund

Figure A.1 / Chart of Accounts. This is a list of all of the accounts in your accounting system. It shows the type of account and relationship between accounts. Your general fund budget will include all of the income and expense accounts identified as general fund accounts.

Church Name

Income and Expenses—General Fund Budget

January 1, 19__ through December 31, 19__

INCOME

Income

400	Regular Offering	$	56000.00
401	Interest Income		400.00
	Total Income		56400.00

TOTAL INCOME	$	56400.00

EXPENSE

Expense

600	Staff Salaries	$	14500.00
601	Staff Car Allowance		3000.00
602	Staff Housing Allowance		9000.00
603	Mortgage Payment		10800.00
610	GF Transfer to Missions		5600.00
615	Utilities		8500.00
620	Sunday School Expense		1200.00
625	Building Insurance		1500.00
630	Building Maintenance		1000.00
635	Janitor Supplies		300.00
650	Office Expense		500.00
660	Print/Advertising		500.00
	Total Expense		56400.00

TOTAL EXPENSE	$	56400.00
NET INCOME (LOSS)	$	0.00

Figure A.2 / General Fund Budget. This report shows the general fund budget of income and expenses. The information from a similar report was copied into a word processing program to produce the budget shown in figure 2.1.

Church Name
General Fund—Actual vs. Budget

	03/01/__ 03/31/__ Actual	03/01/__ 03/31/__ Budget	Dollar Variance
INCOME			
Income			
400 Regular Offering	$ 4150.00	$ 4000.00	$ 150.00
401 Interest Income	29.00	30.00	-1.00
Total Income	4179.00	4030.00	149.00
TOTAL INCOME	$ 4179.00	$ 4030.00	$ 149.00
EXPENSE			
Expense			
600 Staff Salaries	$ 1250.00	$ 1250.00	$ 0.00
601 Staff Car Allowance	225.00	250.00	25.00
602 Staff Housing Allowance	750.00	750.00	0.00
603 Mortgage Payment	900.00	900.00	0.00
610 GF Transfer to Missions	415.00	400.00	-15.00
615 Utilities	750.00	800.00	50.00
620 Sunday School Expense	140.00	150.00	10.00
625 Building Insurance	0.00	0.00	0.00
630 Building Maintenance	52.00	50.00	-2.00
635 Janitor Supplies	35.00	50.00	15.00
650 Office Expense	50.00	50.00	0.00
660 Print/Advertising	0.00	0.00	0.00
Total Expense	4567.00	4650.00	83.00
TOTAL EXPENSE	$ 4567.00	$ 4650.00	$ 83.00
NET INCOME (LOSS)	$ -388.00	$ -620.00	$ 232.00

Figure A.3 / Actual vs. Budget Report Showing Variance in Dollars. This report shows the actual income and disbursements for March compared to the budgeted income and disbursements for the same month. The difference between the two is shown in dollar amounts.

Church Name
General Fund—Actual vs. Budget

	03/01/__ 03/31/__ Actual	03/01/__ 03/31/__ Budget	Dollar Variance	Percent Variance
INCOME				
Income				
400 Regular Offering	$ 4150.00	$ 4000.00	$ 150.00	3.75%
401 Interest Income	29.00	30.00	-1.00	-3.33%
Total Income	4179.00	4030.00	149.00	3.70%
TOTAL INCOME	$ 4179.00	$ 4030.00	$ 149.00	3.70%
EXPENSE				
Expense				
600 Staff Salaries	$ 1250.00	$ 1250.00	$ 0.00	0.00%
601 Staff Car Allowance	225.00	250.00	25.00	10.00%
602 Staff Housing Allowance	750.00	750.00	0.00	0.00%
603 Mortgage Payment	900.00	900.00	0.00	0.00%
610 GF Transfer to Missions	415.00	400.00	-15.00	-3.75%
615 Utilites	750.00	800.00	50.00	6.25%
620 Sunday School Expense	140.00	150.00	10.00	6.67%
625 Building Insurance	0.00	0.00	0.00	0.00%
630 Building Maintenance	52.00	50.00	-2.00	-4.00%
635 Janitor Supplies	35.00	50.00	15.00	30.00%
650 Office Expense	50.00	50.00	0.00	0.00%
660 Print/Advertising	0.00	0.00	0.00	0.00%
Total Expense	4567.00	4650.00	83.00	1.78%
TOTAL EXPENSE	$ 4567.00	$ 4650.00	$ 83.00	1.78%
NET INCOME (LOSS)	$ -388.00	$ -620.00	$ 232.00	37.42%

Figure A.4 / Actual vs. Budget Report Showing Variance in Both Dollars and Percent.
This report compares the actual income and disbursements for March to the budgeted amounts just like the report in figure A.3. You will notice the similarity between these reports and the budget comparison report in figure 5.1.

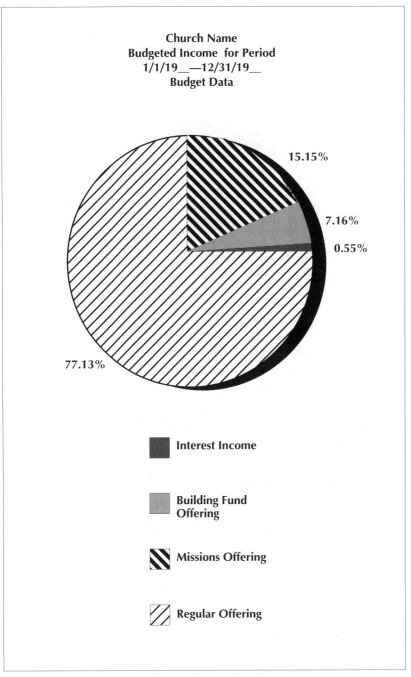

**Church Name
Budgeted Income for Period
1/1/19___—12/31/19___
Budget Data**

15.15%

7.16%

0.55%

77.13%

■ Interest Income

▨ Building Fund Offering

◼ Missions Offering

▨ Regular Offering

Figure A.5 / Pie Chart, Distribution of Annual Budgeted Income. This chart is produced from the information included in the computer's records of the budgeted income for a church. The information graphically illustrates the expectations about the amount of income for the year from each source.

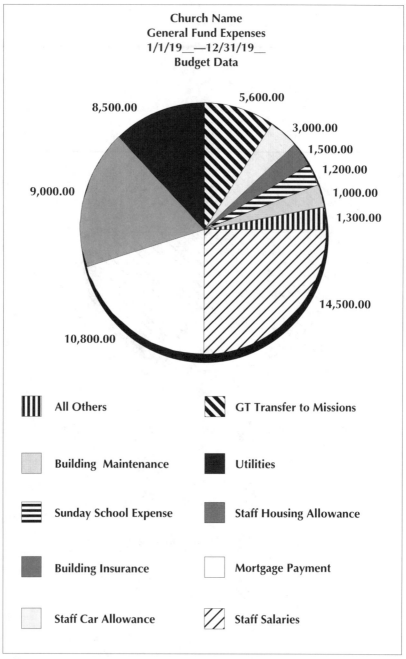

Figure A.6 / Pie Chart, Distribution of Annual Budgeted Expense. This chart is similar to figure A.5 except it shows expenses and the distribution shown by the pie slices is in dollars rather than percent.

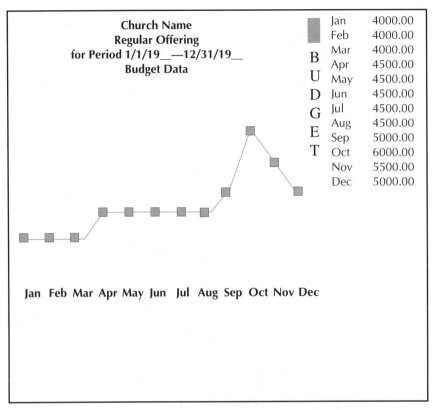

Figure A.7 / Line Graph Depicting Monthly Budgeted Income. This graph presents a visual picture of the expected total income for each month of the year. The fact that a variation in income is expected from month to month is easily seen. The side panel shows the budgeted amounts for each month.

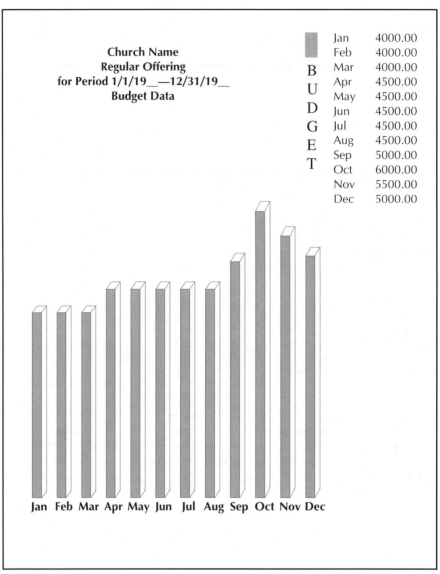

Church Name
Regular Offering
for Period 1/1/19__—12/31/19__
Budget Data

B
U
D
G
E
T

Jan	4000.00
Feb	4000.00
Mar	4000.00
Apr	4500.00
May	4500.00
Jun	4500.00
Jul	4500.00
Aug	4500.00
Sep	5000.00
Oct	6000.00
Nov	5500.00
Dec	5000.00

Jan Feb Mar Apr May Jun Jul Aug Sep Oct Nov Dec

Figure A.8 / Bar Graph Depicting Monthly Budgeted Income. This graph shows the same information as figure A.7 but in a different format. Notice the expected growth in church size and income discussed in chapter 4 are visually depicted. Personal preference will determine which graph you will use.

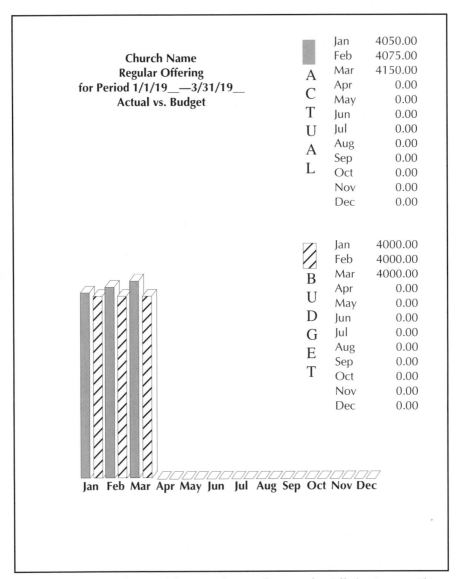

Church Name
Regular Offering
for Period 1/1/19__—3/31/19__
Actual vs. Budget

A
C
T
U
A
L

Jan	4050.00
Feb	4075.00
Mar	4150.00
Apr	0.00
May	0.00
Jun	0.00
Jul	0.00
Aug	0.00
Sep	0.00
Oct	0.00
Nov	0.00
Dec	0.00

B
U
D
G
E
T

Jan	4000.00
Feb	4000.00
Mar	4000.00
Apr	0.00
May	0.00
Jun	0.00
Jul	0.00
Aug	0.00
Sep	0.00
Oct	0.00
Nov	0.00
Dec	0.00

Jan Feb Mar Apr May Jun Jul Aug Sep Oct Nov Dec

Figure A.9 / Bar Graph Comparing Actual vs. Budget Regular Offering Income. This graph shows the relationship between the actual and the budgeted regular offering in a pictorial fashion. The side panel shows the figures for both the actual and the budgeted amounts and makes the graph more informative.

Appendix B

Converting Goals
to Budgets

In chapter 2 we discussed the importance of setting goals and establishing priorities for them as the beginning point in the budgeting process. This appendix illustrates how that is accomplished.

The assumptions, goals, priorities, and decisions reflected in this appendix are for the purpose of illustration only and are not related to any previous chart, graph, or figure. Your church may have specific circumstances and goals that would cause you to make different decisions from those made here, but this illustration still should be helpful. It demonstrates the process of converting goals to budgets, not just the final outcome.

Goals

Two goals will be used in this example. They are:

1. Contingency Fund (Reserve). Set aside money in a contingency fund equal to one month's General Fund Offering by the end of the fiscal year. This fund is to be used only for emergencies.

2. Begin Paying the Pastor. Begin paying the pastor by paying his ministry expenses and other personal benefits.

Discussion of Contingency Fund Goal

A contingency fund, sometimes called a reserve fund, is often maintained to ensure that the church can handle unexpected (unbudgeted) expenses without having to borrow money or become delinquent in paying normal expenses. The size of the contingency fund depends on how much risk the pastor and congregation can feel comfortable with. If the pastor believes he can raise special offerings to cover most emergencies, then the amount kept in this fund can be small or nonexistent. If the congregation is made up of people who already give sacrificially and do not have the capacity to give substantial additional amounts of money on short notice, and who also have very low tolerance for financial risk, then the size of the contingency fund needs to be significantly larger.

Another factor that affects the size of the contingency fund is the stated purpose for which it can be used. In the goal statement above, the contingency fund can be used only for emergencies. The church might want to change the authorized use of this fund to include "smoothing out" the monthly general fund income. To do this, they could authorize the contingency fund to be used as a "line of credit." (A line of credit is simply an open-ended, short-term loan that can be drawn on at any time.) Usually, a line of credit must be paid back entirely at a point in time each year. If the contingency fund were to be used as a line of credit to make up for temporary short-falls in general fund income, then the amount of money planned to be kept in the fund would probably need to be larger than if it is only to be used for emergencies.

In this illustration, your goal is to build a fund that can only be used for emergencies, so building it large enough to be used as a line of credit is not a consideration. However, if your plan was to use it as a line of credit, you could look at an early draft of the cash flow budget to determine the amount you would need in the contingency fund to cover expected monthly deficits caused by the timing of income and expenses. By adding the largest expected cumulative deficit (see fig. 4.2) to the amount you need for emergencies, you can compute the total amount needed in the fund. You will also notice that the cash flow budget in figure 4.2 shows months with surpluses as well as with deficits, so the line of credit borrowing from the contingency fund can be paid back by the end of the fiscal year.

When you consider establishing and building this fund, remember that what you put into it is not an expense. Deposits into the contingency fund are transfers of cash assets from the general fund into a different fund that is also a repository for cash assets. You "spend" it out of the general fund that you use for paying the church's ordinary expenses, but the money never leaves the bank account. The money remains in your bank account for you to spend; you have merely restricted its use by deciding to spend it only for emergencies.

In your goal statement, you stated the desire to build the account over the course of the year to an amount equal to one month's general fund offering. If you are estimating an increase in income throughout the course of the year, you will need to decide how much money is equal to one month's income because the estimated income will vary from month to month. In any event, you must decide on an exact dollar amount for your goal so that figure can be included in your budget.

Remember that after you have built the contingency fund to the size you want, you do not need to continue putting money into it. However, if an emergency arises that takes money out of the fund, you will need to replenish it by making monthly "payments" into it again. To preclude on-again-off-again transfers into the contingency fund, you might want to budget a set amount to be transferred into the fund each month and consider that amount to be discretionary income in months when it is not needed to maintain the desired balance (see p. 20).

In many small churches, starting a contingency fund to cover emergencies is almost an impossible dream, and building a fund to allow the luxury of borrowing from it is beyond the realm of possibility. However, if the goal to start such a fund is never considered, it will never be created and funded regardless of the size of the church or how long it has been established.

Discussion of Paying the Pastor Goal

This goal (see p. 106) assumes that this is a relatively new church trying to make it possible for the pastor to work full-time in church ministry without having a secular job to support his family. Many new or struggling churches include a salary for the pastor in their budget, but when the weekly offerings are down, they pay the other bills and skip the pastor's salary. They may even keep a record of how much back salary they owe the pastor, but that does not put groceries on his table nor pay his family expenses. Since the pastor is in his position because of a spiritual calling rather than because he is a hired employee, he often accepts not being paid regularly as a part of "being in the ministry." Even though the pastor accepts the conditions, it does not make it right. Paying the pastor's salary is just as important as paying the utility bills. Not paying the pastor when some form of pay has been promised sets a poor example for the church and the community, and nullifies the church's implied claim to moral integrity.

When a church starts planning to pay the pastor, they should plan to start with an amount that they can continue, even during difficult times. The pastor's pay should be like any other budget item being considered. If the amount being considered has a high enough priority when compared to other ministries and budget items, it should be included—if it does not, it should not.

If the goal is to begin supporting the pastor by paying the most that is possible, given the church's current status, it may be that the church will have to start by paying less than a full-time salary. If they must start this way (this is not unusual when starting a new congregation), they might also plan to review the pastor's pay at regular intervals and consider making appropriate budget revisions.

It may be good to think in terms of benefits rather than salary because there are benefits that generally make up the total salary package for a pastor. It may be possible to begin paying the pastor by budgeting to fund only one or two of the parts. Whatever the starting amount is, it should be an amount that is decided on while considering all other potential budget items and their priorities.

To illustrate the point, the church might decide to begin supporting their pastor by paying his car expenses. Car expenses will be one of the major expenses he will incur as long as he is in the ministry. He usually must purchase and maintain a car that is dependable so he can make all of the hospital calls, personal calls in the members' homes, and evangelistic calls that are part of his duties. Having a dependable car requires oil changes and repairs, new tires and windshield wipers, tune-ups, license plates, and car insurance as well as the original investment. Pastors sometimes drive thirty to forty thousand miles each year, three to four times as much as many members of their congregations.

Goal number 2 is to begin paying ministry-related expenses, and paying the pastor's car expenses is a good beginning point. If he is required to submit documentation to the church to support his claim for reimbursement of his transportation costs, and the church does not pay him more than twenty-nine cents per mile (in 1995), then the pastor does not even have to report the amount he is paid for his car expenses on his federal income tax form.

Beginning to pay the pastor with an arrangement like this allows him to keep 100 percent of what the church pays him. If the same amount were paid to him as salary, a part of it would probably be paid out in income taxes. Although twenty-nine cents per mile might not completely cover the cost of operating some cars, it is a good starting point.

The same type of tax advantages can be gained by paying for the pastor's health insurance and by providing him with a housing allowance to pay for his rent, or mortgage payment, and utility costs. Since every dollar paid to the pastor in these ways stays with him to help support his family and himself in the ministry, the church provides more actual financial benefits to the pastor by starting his salary package by paying for these expenses first.

Each of these expenses, taken by itself, is a relatively small portion of the total salary package the church may desire to eventually pay their pastor. By planning to begin to pay for one type of expense at a time, the church is able to make small, incremental, but legitimate, commitments toward paying their pastor. By paying for an increasing number of these identifiable portions of a total "salary package," the church is able to work toward paying their pastor adequately so he can be engaged in full-time ministry. They can compensate their pastor appropriately without having to promise the whole package at one time and risking not being able to keep their promise.

Prioritizing Goals

Each of these goals must be considered in relation to the entire budget. It is obvious that paying the rent or mortgage and the utility bills for the church should have a higher priority than establishing a contingency fund. In a new church it is also probable that paying those bills would have a higher priority than paying the pastor because he is probably there with the express intention of serving without pay until the church grows.

However, the priority given to the pastor's pay should go up once the church begins paying him.

Remember, a list of written goals is merely a wish list until you assign each of them a priority so you can work to achieve them. If you are to do the most important things with the church's income, you must decide which goals are the most important.

Estimating Amounts for Each Goal

Estimating the amount needed to build a contingency fund equal to one month's general fund income within one year is simple and straightforward. If your estimated monthly general fund income is determined to be $4,200, then you will need to set aside $350 per month to reach your goal ($4,200 ÷ 12=$350).

Estimating the amount to set aside to begin paying the pastor is not as easy. If you decide to begin the pastor's salary package by paying some of his expenses that will enable him to enjoy some financial benefits without paying taxes on them, you should start by estimating the cost of each of the expenses. If you plan to pay his car expenses and decide to pay him twenty-nine cents per business mile, then all you have to do is multiply the estimated number of miles he will drive during the course of the year by twenty-nine cents. If he expects to drive fifteen thousand miles on church related business, then you should budget $4,350 for the pastor's car expenses. (15,000 miles x 29¢/mile=$4,350)

After computing the amount it will cost to pay the pastor's car expenses, you might decide that you cannot afford to pay all of them. You might decide, for example, that when all of the higher priority expenses are considered, you can only afford to pay $250 per month toward the pastor's car expenses. If that is the best you can do under the current circumstances, then you can specify that the church will pay twenty-nine cents per mile for car expenses up to $250 per month. By doing this you:

- Achieve the goal of starting to pay the pastor.
- Treat this budget expense the same as all others

so you can do the most important things with your income.

- Have made a promise to the pastor that he can count on and which will allow the church to maintain its good name for honest dealing.

On the other hand, you might find that after considering all higher priority expenses, you have $7,500 per year that can be used for paying the pastor. In this case, you can plan to pay him for all of his estimated ministry miles and still have $3,150 remaining to pay other expenses. You might decide to pay for his medical insurance or begin paying him a housing allowance. What you do will depend on the particular circumstances of the pastor and the church. In either case, you can achieve your stated budget goal.

After making the estimates for each of these goals, it is a simple procedure to include them in your annual budget and cash flow budget as illustrated in chapters 2 and 4.

Appendix C

Written Procedures for Church Budgeting

Written procedures for developing and operating church budgets help guide the budget development and control process, provide direction for new members of the financial management team, and act as a checklist to preclude overlooking important actions. Although small churches with only the pastor, or the pastor and one or two others, involved may not need written procedures as much as larger churches with many people involved, they are still helpful.

Since the budget development cycle comes around only once a year, it is hard to remember what you did last year unless it is written down. There is no need to reinvent the wheel each year, so writing a brief outline of the procedures you use will save you time and effort every year when you start the budget development process. It will help you during the year, too, while you are actively involved in operating and staying within your budget's guidelines.

The Church Budget Procedures Guide in this appendix will help you develop your own written procedures. Make changes in it as needed to adapt it to your church.

Church Budget Procedures Guide

Budgeting Responsibilities

The budget is a plan for financing approved ministries of _____ Church. All financial decisions of the pastor and church board will give priority to activities and functions related to the ministries of the church. This includes the budget development process as well as authorization of actual expenditures. The church fiscal year is January 1 through December 31.

The pastor, in coordination with the budget committee (or church board), is responsible for the development of the annual budget proposal that is presented to the church for their approval. After church approval, he (or the business manager if there is one) is responsible for operating the church in accordance with the approved budget and for recommending budget revisions when necessary.

The budget committee is appointed in accordance with the church bylaws. Assignments to specific duties within the committee are made by the pastor. This committee assists the pastor in estimating the income for the new budget year and evaluating and assigning priorities to the budget requests submitted by ministry leaders.

Ministry leaders are responsible to the pastor and are assigned to plan and manage the budget for income and expense accounts that affect their area of ministry. Incumbents in the following positions are designated ministry leaders: youth minister, bus director, Sunday School department superintendents, etc. (List all positions whose incumbents are assigned sufficient responsibility for the control of supplies, equipment, or funds to warrant their inclusion in the budget process.)

Budget Development Procedures

a. On or about October 1st each year, the pastor will ask each ministry leader to review each item on his department's budget and prepare to make recommendations related to them at a budget meeting with the pastor, the budget committee (church board), and other ministry leaders. Ministry leaders who desire major budget changes will submit their requests and justification for their desired changes to the pastor on the standard Budget Request Form (fig. 3.1) at least one week prior to the meeting. Major budget changes include adding new items, major changes in requested amounts for items currently in the budget (either increase or decrease), or deletion of items.

b. The first meeting of the budget committee and all ministry leaders will be conducted during mid-October. General guidelines for the next budget year will be discussed at this meeting as well as the major budget changes requested by the ministry leaders.

c. The date for final submission of each ministry leader's budget will be decided at the first budget meeting. (This date is usually about two weeks after the first budget meeting.) Final submission of budget requests based on revisions suggested and instructions given at the first meeting with the budget committee and ministry leaders will be made on the standard Budget Request Form (fig. 3.1). Requests must contain complete justification for every budget item, the basis for computing the amount requested, and the suggested timing of the expenditure or receipt of income.

d. The pastor will consolidate all requests and make a preliminary annual budget and a monthly cash-flow budget for review by the budget committee at a meeting in early November. He will ensure that the justification submitted by each ministry leader for each budget item is available for reference at this meeting. Changes suggested or necessitated after reviewing the information submitted by the ministry leaders will be discussed and approved or disapproved by the budget committee and pastor by mid-November.

e. The format for the annual budget proposal includes the previous year's budget, the current year's budget, and the new year's budget as shown in attachment #___. (You should develop a sample budget similar to the one shown in fig. 2.1 and attach it to your Church Budget Procedures Guide. Insert the attachment number you assign it.) The format for the cash flow budget based on the proposed annual budget will show the monthly expectations for each item of income and expense as shown in attachment #___. (Attach a sample cash flow budget and insert its assigned attachment number. Use fig. 4.1 as a guide.)

f. The approved budget will be coordinated with the ministry leaders at a joint meeting with the budget committee and pastor in late November. (Note: If the church bylaws require church board approval before the budget is submitted to the church, it should be done at this time.)

g. The date for a church business meeting to approve the new budget will be set and publicized in accordance with church bylaws. One copy of the proposed budget will be posted on the church bulletin board and additional copies made available in the church office.

h. The pastor will present the proposed budget to the church for approval at the business meeting called for that purpose. The approved budget will become effective at the beginning of the new fiscal year.

Operating Procedures

a. The pastor (business manager) will meet monthly with appropriate ministry leaders to review the prior month's actual cash-flow and determine the cause of any deviations from the cash-flow budget. They will also review the financial progress for the current month and discuss expected deviations from the budget projection for the month following.

b. Purchase orders must be approved for all purchases even though the item requested is included in the approved budget. This procedure ensures that budget provisions are reviewed by each appropriate ministry leader and the pastor before expenditures are approved.

c. Some budgeted items, such as office supplies and building maintenance, require great leeway for the appropriate manager so he/she can make routine purchases without seeking approval for many small or unplanned purchase orders. When necessary in such cases, the pastor will approve an "open purchase order" for the appropriate manager for specific budget items. He will assign specific dollar limits for each item. When this is done, the manager may make purchases for the specifically approved budget item up to the approved limit. Purchases that will result in monthly expenditures above the "open purchase order" limit must be approved in advance by the pastor.

d. Purchase order requests may be originated by any church worker or staff member. After furnishing all of the required information on the purchase order form (fig. 6.2), the originator will sign the form and submit it to the appropriate ministry leader. The ministry leader will review the form for completeness and accuracy, and ensure that it is within his approved budget limit. If he is satisfied that the purchase order request is appropriate and in accordance with the approved budget, he will sign it and forward it to the pastor for final approval.

e. No purchase can be made without an approved purchase order. No purchase order is approved until the pastor (or business manager) signs it.

f. The ministry leader will ensure that all purchase orders approved or completed for his or her department are entered into the purchase order log.

Long Range Financial Planning

It is important to establish long-range goals in order to guide short-range planning. Ministry leaders should maintain a list of long range goals for their departments which will include suggested times for the accomplishment of each goal. When developing these goals, ministry leaders will consider personnel, equipment, buildings, and time requirements. These goals will be consolidated and discussed at a meeting of the pastor and all ministry leaders in the fall of each year, before the beginning of the next budget development cycle. The results of this meeting will be used in developing and revising the church's long-range plan.